Michelle

D1099165

The Pocket Essential

JACKIE CHAN

Thanks for everything

Love Colin & Mike

www.pocketessentials.com

First published in Great Britain 2000 by Pocket Essentials, 18 Coleswood Rd, Harpenden, Herts, AL5 1EQ

Distributed in the U.S.A. by Trafalgar Square Publishing, P.O.Box 257, Howe Hill Rd, North Pomfret, Vermont 05053

A CIP catalogue record for this book is available from the British Library.

ISBN 1-903047-10-2

9 8 7 6 5 4 3 2 1

Book typeset by DP Fact & Fiction.
Printed and bound by Cox & Wyman

To Andy, Lizbeth and Paul, for all the fun we've had at those Hong Kong Triple Bills

Acknowledgements

Huge thanks to the following people for all their assistance and encouragement throughout the writing of this book, particularly those who helped fill the gaps in our video collection: Paul Duncan, Andrew M Butler, Moira Shearman, Paul & Elizabeth Billinger and John Ashbrook. For building our very first video shelves, thanks to Martin Harlow. Thanks also to Sensei Geoff Stansfield of the FSKI for turning our enthusiasm for martial arts into reality. Finally to Alice, who practices the Tiger Claw technique on our sofa.

Contents

1: "I Just Do It"

He's handcuffed. Hanging three stories high from the perilous minute hand of a clocktower. Behind him are axe-wielding maniacs, below are the police. There's nowhere to go but down...

"I've always loved Hollywood's black-and-white silent classics - the comedies of Keaton and Lloyd and Chaplin that, even after decades, continue to make people smile, scream, and laugh."
Jackie Chan (*I Am Jackie Chan*)

Jackie Chan makes people smile, scream, and laugh the world over. He is the world's greatest, most popular action star. But he is far more than that, he is a choreographic innovator on par with Gene Kelly or Fred Astaire, a comic genius like Keaton or Lloyd, an astute director and an unsurpassed entertainer. When you go to see a Jackie Chan film you go to be entertained. His films are infectious. He is an auteur.

Whenever anyone watches a Jackie Chan film, it is the 'gasp factor' that makes the first impression. There are so many fantastic, unbelievable and outrageous scenes, you can end up reeling from it all. Jackie's ace card is the fact that he performs almost all of his own stunts, and that these are nothing short of spectacular. Hollywood action films cheat and are proud to admit it in their cheesy documentaries - where stuntmen double for the star, and the movies employ 'safe techniques' such as careful editing and blue screening (where the action is filmed in front of a screen in the studio and the danger projected onto it). You *know* that Jackie executes his own stunts because he makes sure the camera films his face as he risks life and limb for our entertainment. He is not reckless in this, but his dedication to the stunt image has placed him in danger many times. With such a long career (coming up to forty years!) accidents are inevitable. He has been injured so many times he has lost count, and he almost died on *Armour Of God* when he fell from a tree, hitting his head on a rock. Injuries don't deter him though, a true professional he carries on filming regardless. When he broke his ankle on *Rumble In The Bronx*, rather than let it heal naturally, he wore a fake trainer over the plaster cast and continued shooting.

One of the trademarks of Jackie's films is that of showing the out-takes during the final credits of his films. During these, you will often see the most painful and unpleasant scenes that have up till that point been denied the viewer. Jackie's out-takes accentuate his bond with the audience - they tie him to the real world and make people appreciate the pains to which he has gone to create his entertainment. But they're often really funny too!

There are certain techniques he uses to enhance the stunt and martial arts fight scenes, but very strongly believes that the action must look realistic. Many Hong Kong films, particularly in the fantasy genre, rely heavily on impressively overstylised wirework for their impact. Jackie too uses wires, but in a subtle manner that in many instances actually makes the action more dangerous for the performers, not less! The point is that even though he enhances his stunts, you genuinely believe that he is performing them - anyone, with enough money, can make a dangerous looking film using computer graphics, but Jackie dares to do the real thing. The choice of stunts means that neither he nor his team of stuntmen can get insurance - Jackie's now sizeable fortune takes care of any unfortunate mishaps. Good popular cinema relies on the suspension of disbelief to allow the audience to empathise with their on-screen heroes - the immediacy, human frailty and universality of Chan's characters creates a bond with the viewer that is unsurpassed in modern cinema.

You may watch a Jackie Chan film just for the action and expect no more from him, but in fact closer examination of his work reveals a very talented film-maker. He has a particular vision, both with the style and ideology of his productions. Although his films may appear simple, many are quite complex, and while perhaps not offering the most cerebral of challenges, are thoroughly enjoyable and certainly bear several viewings. What are the fundamental ingredients to a Jackie Chan film? They essentially boil down to action and comedy in equal measures, with various conflicts or tragedies along the way. The plots within Jackie's films are usually reasonably straightforward and are certainly less confusing than many Hong Kong films. Western audiences often have trouble understanding plot nuances within HK films, partly because of cultural differences and sometimes because the subtitling or dubbing is poor. Oh, and some really are just plain barmy. Jackie's films develop basic plots and use the action, situation and characterisation to carry the film, which can lead to a rich and sometimes quite complex work. This means that the films can be enjoyed at many levels. Rather than creating intricate stories, several plot strands tend to form, but are often not developed to a great extent - for example love interest is usually present but not developed, Jackie being more likely to get a slap than a snog. It is interesting to note that some Western prints are different to the originals, with some narrative threads cut completely from a particular film.

Jackie considers his films to be suitable for family viewing. To this end, his own productions feature no sex or swearing. Despite the fact that his films may appear exceptionally violent, he considers this to be a 'wholesome' violence, without gratuitous blood or gore, but painful consequences for all concerned. You may want him to win, but you wouldn't want to get involved in a Jackie Chan fight; although he always justifies the fisticuffs within the context of the film. He places emphasis on the act of fighting, employing a funny, fast and acrobatic style. His brawls always depict energy and exuberance over brute force. He also uses his environment to full effect - the playground's climbing frames in *Police Story II* or the gang's den in *Rumble In The Bronx*, so that the fight sometimes becomes almost abstract. Whichever way it's filmed, it always packs real punch.

Jackie's hero is a good guy. He may be flawed and undisciplined, he is certainly tough and his methods may be unorthodox, but he has a strong moral sense and knows right from wrong. If he's part of an institution (a cop or sailor) he bends the rules, with the ends often justifying the means. What is very important to understand is that his heroes hurt too. Early kung fu films usually depict a stoic protagonist who will stand up to his foes or die bravely. Jackie's heroes take the knocks, but always show that even though they are tough, the punches they dish out and receive really hurt. There are two angles to this – one showing that violence is not necessarily a solution to problems, with the other adding pure comedy to the proceedings. In *Project A*, when Ma and Tsu fight, they both hit each other hard and fast, but have to retreat behind a wall to nurse their wounds, before reapplying the bravado and facing each other again. Jackie's later work often reveals more complex characterisation. He may have inner conflicts like Ka-Kui in *Police Story 2* who has to balance his loyalties to the police force and his girlfriend, whilst dealing with explosives dealers and his nemesis. Or he may not be a particularly nice good guy, like CN Chan of *Gorgeous*, who is rich, cynical, ruthless in business and doesn't understand love. Similarly, Tad of *Heart Of Dragon* wants to become a sailor, but has to sacrifice his dreams in order to care for his brother. There are two different sorts of bad guys and they are generally straightforward in their characterisation – the misunderstood youths, who generally learn the errors of their ways, contrast with the evil criminals/corrupt pillars of society, who will genuinely stop at nothing to realise their dastardly deeds. There are few overt political statements within his films - arch bad guys may well be capitalists, but their evil is understandable to all. Likewise, Jackie is careful not to offend religious/social sensibilities. This has allowed his films to be distributed and enjoyed in countries where many other foreign films are banned or frowned upon.

Chan's comedy is of the old school - it is fast, predominantly visual and therefore universal. He often borrows from the silent stars Buster Keaton, Charlie Chaplin and Harold Lloyd, who pioneered a structure of cinematic visual comedy that is rarely seen nowadays. They are worthy of particular comparison because they too carried out their own awesome stunts. Silent cinema had to develop specific techniques in order to portray funny or silly events, because there were no means to produce the fast one-liner, upon which modern comedies often rely. These include overemphasis of movements and facial expressions, something that Jackie uses in both his comedy and martial arts. Much of this has derived from his opera school training, where he performed expressively for the stage. Part of the international appeal to Jackie's films is the fact that his slapstick gags are instantly understandable and genuinely funny to anyone who isn't an angst-ridden teenager. He also uses his body to produce jokes - no matter which culture you are from, everyone can understand a fart gag. But he is also very talented at setting up situation comedy and farce, Marx Brothers style - *Project A Part 2* being of particular note, where several sets of people turn up at the same house and one protagonist must try and prevent them all from meeting. *Dragons Forever* also features Jackie trying to entertain and charm his leading lady, whilst preventing his 'friends' from fighting each other in the other rooms of the apartment.

Not only is Jackie a talented actor, stuntman and choreographer, he also directs his films and has a good deal of control over how they are shot. He is a perfectionist and will reshoot a take several times in order to produce exactly the right effect, even if the shot is on screen for the briefest of moments. Shots in *First Strike* of Jackie jumping through the rungs of a ladder, and in the fight with a fan in *Young Master*, took over 1000 attempts each. The hacky sack match in *Dragon Lord*, was also notorious for the number of takes required to meet Jackie's standards. But this is precisely why his films are so spectacular. Jackie has been known to spend the best part of a year shooting some of his films - fight sequences alone can take months, which is why they look so good. In *Rush Hour* he had one evening to shoot the opening scene, not nearly enough time to produce perfect action. The results are impressive, but it is clear they could have been so much more. The emphasis on getting the action perfect is at odds with Hollywood's reliance on dialogue.

As a director, Jackie favours a mix of styles. He has developed his own methods of filming and editing too. Generally Hong Kong films are paced very speedily with quick cutting between shots, that until very recently made Hollywood action films look positively pedestrian. Jackie has taken this one stage further. He compensates for relatively static camera set ups by cutting around the action very quickly during the fight scenes. Alteration of camera speed is another characteristic of his work. Jackie doesn't merely use slow motion for high impact kicks or wounds. Instead his inspiration seems to have come from Peckinpah's mastery of the film speed, most famously in *The Wild Bunch* (1969). Jackie treats these alterations of time as ways of emphasising the action – the slow, deliberate agony of a head smashed into glass in *Police Story*, the madcap rescue of a puppy among falling furniture in *Who Am I?* or the ritualised climax of *The Young Master* – all have a different kind of audience impact, but rely on the elasticity of time. Nowhere is this more apparent than in the numerous set-piece stunt sequences where the utter lunacy of the death-defying feat is shown not only using different speeds, but from varying angles. The stunts are always filmed with multiple camera set-ups, mainly with the aim of catching the stunt first time - after all, some of these are never to be repeated. But they also provide Chan with a very rich source of material from which he can choose his final cut and, from these perspectives, he can use the shots to enhance the effect. One method he uses is to repeat the same shot in rapid succession, giving the audience the chance to catch the action twice, whilst adding impact. Another technique involves extending the length of the stunt, by intercutting the same action but from different angles, also creating a slight overlap in the actual time each shot plays.

Jackie's insistence on the widescreen (1:2.35 aspect) format allows for a more epic feel - he has often expressed his admiration for David Lean's *Lawrence Of Arabia* (1962) with its sweeping vistas and Robert Wise's *The Sound Of Music* (1965), another film that fills the screen. *Operation Condor* goes for this approach, as does *Who Am I?* The widescreen format generally works better with slow roaming or static camerawork, as over-editing can cause disorientation with the viewer, which is why it's regularly adopted in the action genre. Jackie fills his frame using techniques from silent cinema and the traditional kung fu movie. In these films, the expanse of the screen expresses the gulf between protagonists, the scale of a large melee or merely contains a moving fight sequence. Deriving partly from Chinese opera, there is a sense in which the movements of the characters have to be shown uninterrupted by edits - effectively using the screen as a stage. Jackie takes from both of these styles but keeps in the spirit of the early cinema comics. A long take illustrates to the audience that he is not tricking them, but the power of editing emphasises the immediacy of the action. He has experimented with a more fluid Golden Age Hollywood floating camera style in his sentimental masterpiece *Miracles*, which features some remarkable crane shots and prowling cameras – pure musical. In the same film he uses Busby Berkley-style kaleidoscope shots that re-emphasise his love of traditional Hollywood. All of these reveal the same basic aims – to entertain the audience and to make them believe in his magic.

Notes On Using This Book:

Names can be of some confusion to those dipping their toes into the waters of Hong Kong cinema. Generally we have adopted the principle of using the full name when first mentioned and subsequently the more commonly used name. Matters are not helped by differing spellings (Samo/Sammo Hung, Jet Li/Lee) and alternative names formed by distributors or even the stars themselves. Jackie himself has gone through a fair number - in the past he has been credited as Jacky and Chan Yuen Lung.

Each film mentioned has been given two ratings - one for the actual film quality itself and also a Chan rating, which indicates the extent to which it contains all the elements essential to a Jackie Chan film.

2: Painted Faces

Jackie Chan was born Chan Kong Sang, which means 'Born in Hong Kong,' in April 1954. He was twelve months inside the womb and weighed a whopping 12lb at birth. His parents had both been forced to leave China and his name reflected their hopes for the future. Charles, his father, was a cook at the French Embassy and his mother, Lee-Lee a housekeeper. He had a loving upbringing, but his parents were very poor. When he was seven, his father was offered a position at the American Embassy in Australia, but couldn't afford to take the family. Instead, he enrolled Jackie at Sifu Yu Jim-Yuen's China Drama Academy for ten years. Life at the opera school was incredibly tough, the children learned acrobatics, dance, singing, fighting and would train from 5am to midnight, developing the skills that would enable them to perform in the dramatic Peking Operas. The film *Painted Faces* nostalgically depicts the life of the students - Master Yuen's role was played by Jackie's Biggest Brother at the school, Samo Hung Kam Bo (best known in the West for the TV series *Martial Law*). Although it shouldn't be considered biographical, it does focus on Jackie (called Big Nose) and contains many of the stories that Jackie relayed in his autobiography. Jackie was a good all-rounder and was selected to become one of Master Yuen's Seven Little Fortunes (along with Samo and Yuen Biao) who performed opera at the Lai Yuen Amusement Park. However, interest in traditional Chinese opera was beginning to dwindle in the 60s, so young Jackie was called upon to act in some of the films that were being made at the time, and this is how he found his way into the film industry. The legacy of Master Yuen lies with some of Hong Kong cinema's biggest stars - many of his pupils took his name as a sign of respect, and you'd be hard pressed not to find a Yuen in the credits of most HK films. When Jackie left the school, it was about to close down, so he decided to become a stuntman. Success, however, was a long way off.

Early Films (1962-1971)

Director: Various

Cast: Various

Plot: You killed my father/brother/Sifu. Or you dishonoured my mother/sister/martial arts school. Ha ha ha. Compulsory training session. Thwap! Thunk! The end.

Comment: Stuntmen in Hong Kong were hired on a daily basis at the studio gates and did not enjoy the privileges of a union, regular work or accident pay. Only the hardiest, most foolish and luckiest got regular work and recognition. Jackie became accepted in this world because he took risks, something he still does today. Because of the tight schedules involved in making a film, and the hire-and-fire attitude towards stuntmen, it meant that our young hero was featured in more pictures than anyone can care to mention, himself included! His progression through the ranks started with the fairly innocuous 'dead body' role ("there's Jackie, fifth corpse from the left"), through to 'dying body' role ("there's Jackie, fifth from the left"), 'falling off things' role, to even more dangerous 'stunt role' and finally 'stunt co-ordinator.' In Hong Kong cinema, the martial arts choreographer or stunt director often has as important a role to play as the director, and young Jackie aspired to this. His rise through the ranks was fairly swift because of a combination of talent, hard work and the highly desired capacity to accept low wages. He also saw the filming process at work, accumulating skills that would put him in good stead later in his career.

That most of Jackie's early performances are lost or forgotten should come as no surprise. The studios were churning out films at a vast rate to satisfy the appetites of audiences - preservation or archiving was not a high priority. All but the most celebrated or fortunate remain. Even before leaving Opera School, the young dragon was performing in films that he never saw. He appeared in a number of films with Li Li-Hua, a famous Taiwanese actress, including *Big And Little Wong Tin-Bar* (1962 – Jackie cites this as his first role at the age of eight) and *The Love Eternal* (1963), the former within a year of starting school. More formative would prove to be his two films as a stuntman/extra for the legendary director King Hu, *Come Drink With Me* (1966) with Cheng Pei-Pei, and *A Touch Of Zen* (1968). These early films are certainly worth a watch but you'd be hard pressed to spot Jackie.

Of more general interest are two films starring Bruce Lee

which also featured Jackie. Bruce Lee needs little introduction, he was the world's most widely-recognised martial arts film star despite appearing in only four completed movies before his untimely death. In 1971, Bruce was working on his second film *Fist Of Fury*, for director Lo Wei. At the climax of the film, the evil sensei is punched through a paper and wooden wall and falls a large distance into a gravel garden outside. This was performed by stunt double Jackie. His bravery (Jackie was knocked temporarily unconscious by the stunt) did not go unnoticed by either Bruce, Lo Wei or future manager Willie Chan, who was scouting on set at the time. Bruce Lee's final completed film was *Enter The Dragon* (1973), an East/West crossover directed by Robert Clouse. Masses of stuntmen were required for the shoot, and apparently Bruce had insisted that Jackie, the guy who went through the wall, was one of them. Shortly after completion, Bruce Lee died. His legacy consisted of hundreds of inferior kung fu flicks made on the cheap, resulting in the West shunning the cinema of the East. It was not until Chan revised the flagging genre by being the antithesis of Bruce Lee's character that matters took a turn for the better.

Little Tiger Of Canton (aka Master With Cracked Fingers) (1971)

Director: Chin Hsin

Cast: Jackie Chan, Juan Hsao Ten, Shih Tien, Han Kuo Tsi, Yuen Bill, Chang Chin, Kuen Yung Man

Plot: Young Jackie, told by his adopted father not to fight, is secretly taught martial arts by a beggar. Years later, his uncle's restaurant is terrorised by an assortment of local thugs. Jackie naturally defends the restaurant and his sister, but is forced to plunge his hands into broken glass for his violent behaviour. Eventually Jackie must face the bad guy who killed his real father.

Comment: Often regarded as Jackie's first film, *Little Tiger Of Canton* shares a common thread with many of his subsequent films, the number of titles associated with it! Considered too poor to be released at the time, the film was revived with additional footage in the light of Jackie's success. To say this is a garbled mess is perhaps an understatement. Your confidence is further questioned by seeing a film 'Starring Jackie Chan' with

'Martial Arts by Chan Yuen Lung,' who is Jackie, using big brother Samo's stage name. *Little Tiger Of Canton* is by anyone's measure a poor film, but there is a spark there that gives an indication of things to come – the martial arts sequences are adequate but when Jackie starts tumbling you can really enjoy his skills. A flowerpot catching routine is particularly impressive and an otherwise lacklustre cliff-top fight is compelling, because you know there are no safety precautions whatsoever. Top of the list though is a dockside brawl where Jackie swings on some rigging and takes out the mob. It looks a bit staged but is well choreographed and imaginative. This film is bad, but at least it's watchably bad - it includes the atrocious fish fighting stance, the wonderfully camp syndicate boss, the treacherous pickpocket, the kung fu sister and that comedy staple - the fart gag. Watch drunk.

Film Rating: ✪
Chan Rating: ✪✪

Jackie was approached to be stunt co-ordinator for the new Da Di (Great Earth) film company. He jumped at the chance and managed to get school buddies Yuen Biao and Yuen Kwan aboard too. Despite the shoddy conditions, it gave Jackie his first chance at directing the action, something he clearly relished.

The Heroine (aka Kung Fu Girl) (1971)

Director: Lo Wei

Cast: Jackie Chan, Cheng Pei-Pei, James Tien

Plot: Our heroine is in Beijing to help the Chinese resistance against the Japanese. Much fighting and tragedy ensues.

Comment: Considering the resources, the results are not too bad although you'd hardly want to watch this twice. Jackie is cast as the most prominent villain, and Japanese to boot so plausibility isn't the key issue here, or acting come to that! Jackie has made worse, perhaps not cheaper though. *The Heroine* was a flop even in Hong Kong.

Film Rating: ✪
Chan Rating: ✪

Eagle Shadow Fist (aka Not Scared To Die) (1973)

Director: Hdeng Tsu

Cast: Jackie Chan, Wang Qing, Lin Xiu

Plot: 1939. Breaking out of a POW camp, two ex-Peking Opera school performers/anti-Japanese resistance fighters find refuge in the home of a Chinese family. Grandfather is ill, his rickshaw business plundered by the local 'Co-Operation Society,' four extortioneers under the command of the traitorous Chairman Chan. The Chairman is a stooge for the evil Japanese general who, with his henchmen, determines to break the resistance.

Comment: Another film for Da Di, like many of his earlier works, it has a reshot title sequence to push the Jackie angle. At least this time Jackie is the good guy, although by playing second lead to Tang, his survival to the final reel is in doubt from the word go. This is one of those pathos-rich revenge tragedies that allows but one survivor.

In order to disguise the lack of money and rehearsal time, the filmmakers adopted a hand held camera approach and a heightened sense of brutality to compensate for the choreography and stylised compositions of the traditional kung fu film. The fights emphasise the hard, slow punch over the lightning quick acrobatics that would characterise Chan's later work. The relentless barrage of atrocities make the film drag somewhat, as the baddies just keep turning up and pasting a few more family members before an angst ridden Tang duffs a few of them up. Jackie does get a couple of fights though and his on-screen action really puts the star to shame - it's about twice as quick. The highlight occurs when Jackie and the granddaughter are jumped by the four hoods. He gets to do some impressive damage before the numbers go against him. Beaten to a bloody pulp, he is impaled with a sword. Dead? Not quite. He survives just long enough to crawl home and spurt out directions before croaking his last. Pass the hankies, please. Sniff.

Eagle Shadow Fist is cheap and nasty but passes the time. Jackie is at least a good guy this time, although his credo of "no blood, only good violence" is lacking in this little number.

Film Rating: ✪✪

Chan Rating: ✪

Police Woman (aka Young Tiger, Rumble In Hong Kong) (1973)

Director: Hdeng Tsu

Cast: Jackie Chan, Chun Cheung Lam

Plot: A couple are attacked by a ruthless gang. The girl lives long enough to hide a purse in a taxi, the driver of which is then harassed by the group. The girl's sister is a police woman and together with the cabby, seeks justice from the drug smuggling gang her errant sister used to work for.

Comment: The final film for Da Di features the fledgling star as lead henchman of the drug baron's gang. Like *The Heroine* it was not a success, the company went bust and Jackie was left without some of the pay owed to him. He was broke.

Hampered by a limited budget and some of the most appalling dubbing ever (at some points they just give up!) there are a couple of adequate fist fights for Jackie to get involved in, and choreograph. When making his escape, Jackie dashes up a corrugated wall and nonchalantly drops down the other side but really that's about as good as it gets. Added to this, for some perverse reason known only to the film-makers, Jackie has been fitted with an amusingly large piece of black carpet on his left cheek - you feel like shouting "Wash your face you dirty pup" the first time, but then you realise it's meant to be there! Later, when recalling his assailants, the taxi driver comments about "the big mole" and suddenly everything becomes clear - it's a stuffed mammal on his face after all!

Film Rating: ✪
Chan Rating: ✪
Mole Rating: ✪✪✪✪✪

The Himalayan (1975)

Director: Huang Feng

Cast: Jackie Chan, Angela Mao, Chen Sing, Tan Tao Liang (aka Dorian Tan or Bruce Liang!), Samo Hung

Plot: With their community overtaken by a vicious dictator, two villagers run to Nepal where they are taught the fighting skills necessary to reclaim their rightful freedom.

Comment: Samo stunt-directed this adequate kung fu film with Jackie taking a couple of high falls for the camera, smashing through a balcony at one point. He has a small additional role, but the film belongs to Angela Mao, Golden Harvest's premiere fighting female of the time who with 'Flash Legs' Tan makes the best of the production.

Film Rating: ✪✪
Chan Rating: ✪

All In The Family (1975)

Director: Chu Mu

Cast: Jackie Chan, Linda Chu, Dean Shek, Samo Hung

Plot: A family is brought together by their dying elder but the reunion is strained by the appearance of a randy, salty rickshaw driver. 'Hilarity and sauciness' abounds.

Comment: A real curiosity piece that until recently was conspicuous by its absence on Jackie's CV. The reason? This is the only film where you get to see Jackie's bottom for non-comedy purposes as he seduces a mother and daughter. Jackie has had only two on-screen sex scenes in his whole career. They're both here and it's clear why the experiment was not repeated! Any claims that this is a Hong Kong version of Passolini's *Theorem* are quickly dispelled by melodramatics and poor production values. Chan is lecherous and unfunny, but mercifully his role in the film is little more than a repeated cameo.

Film Rating: ✪
Chan Rating: ✪

None of the films he had appeared in were successful so, disillusioned, Jackie returned to Australia to join his parents, and briefly worked in construction. However, he couldn't settle down and returned to Hong Kong where big brother Samo helped him to find more film work.

Hand Of Death (1976)

Director: John Woo

Cast: Jackie Chan, Dorien Tan Tian Lung, Samo Hung, Yuen Biao

Plot: Those naughty Manchus are up to no good again, breaking up the Shaolin temple and stealing the secret of the scary Goose Fist technique. To get revenge, Lion needs a map and teams up with Tien, a woodcutter (Jackie), and flute player

Zorro, to perfect their Tiger Claw technique and defeat the dreaded Hawk Style. It's off to the fort for the final showdown, but who will make it out alive?

Comment: Samo had landed himself a job as a choreographer and actor, and managed to get roles for Jackie and Yuen Biao. *Hand Of Death* features the first teaming of the three. It is also an early film from John Woo and although not great, indicates the road ahead. Woo, one time protégé of the prolific Cheng Cheh, would later shoot to fame in Hong Kong with *A Better Tomorrow* (1987) and *Hard Boiled* (1994) before moving to Hollywood, making fantastic big budget films like *Face/Off* (1997). Samo, sporting some of the most ridiculous teeth to grace a baddie, choreographed the fights which vary from pedestrian to electric, but all share a common thread of traditionalism that continues in his work even today. Chan, in his last film prior to eye and teeth surgery, gets a fairly meaty role as the woodcutter. He fights with the best of them, excelling in a table and salt pot smashing routine and generally focusing the plans of revenge. This being 1970s kung fu, the end isn't all roses and our plucky woodcutter is struck down by a Manchu spear. A poignant death scene can be one of the highlights of an actor's career, but not this one. Jackie, a look of surprise on his face, falls like a plank, appropriate for his character perhaps.

The three brothers and Woo have commented on how much fun they had making *Hand Of Death* - they were all young, reckless and out for a good time. No one could expect the success that they would all later achieve.

Injury: Knocked unconscious
Rating: ✪✪✪
Chan Rating: ✪

3: There's No Business Like Lo Business

In 1975, Willie Chan, a talent scout and former general manager at the Cathay Organisation, had just started working for director Lo Wei. At the time Lo, like most Hong Kong directors, wanted to find a successor to Bruce Lee. He had a more vested interest than most, having directed Bruce's first two films, *The Big Boss* (1971) and *Fist Of Fury (1972)*. In seeking a replacement for Lee, Lo Wei and Willie came up with Jackie. Willie would become Jackie's permanent manager, best friend and an essential cog in the Chan machine. Lo Wei would become a serious problem.

New Fist Of Fury (1976)

Director: Lo Wei

Cast: Jackie Chan, Nora Miao, Han Ying Chieh, Chen King

Plot: Following the dissolution of the Ching Yung martial arts school by the Japanese (the end of the first film), the survivors decide to start up a new school in Taiwan. Not a sensible move as Taiwan is also under Japanese occupation. The Japanese want them all to bow to their superior technique but will they do it when rebellious Ah Lung (Jackie) joins the school?

Comment: Imaginatively titled *New Fist of Fury*, the film takes most of its cast and plot from the first film and plunges Jackie slap bang in the middle. The problem with this choice is evident from the start – Jackie is incapable of the brooding angst and bursting aggression that characterised Bruce. He just looks like Jackie, a cheeky chappy with hot martial arts and tumbling skills. Nowhere is this more clear than in the nunchuka sequence where he hits himself with the infamous weapon and does a very quick comedy grimace. Generally, we see Jackie seethe for two hours, spurting out "I hate the Japs" at every opportunity and stumbling from fight to fight. When he finally joins the true Chinese kung fu school, Lo Wei films him like a Christ figure and intercuts this with footage of Bruce Lee to emphasise the similarity! Additionally, in the original, Bruce did a mildly silly multi-hand routine that worked, sadly Jackie just looks drugged.

It is a real shame that this film is so poor because a lot of the supporting cast give wonderful performances. Problems lie in the inflated running time, lacklustre scripting and a disregard for originality or interest. It will come as no surprise to learn that *New Fist Of Fury* was not the record breaking smash that Lo Wei had counted on. A lesson learnt by all? Sadly not…

Injury: Signing a contract with Lo Wei seriously hampered Jackie's career opportunities.

Film Rating: ✪✪

Chan Rating: ✪

Shaolin Wooden Men (1976)

Director: Chen Chi-Hwa

Cast: Jackie Chan, Simon Yuen, Lung Chung-Erh, Kam Kan

Plot: Dummy (Jackie), a mute Shaolin disciple, works to improve his kung fu in order to leave the monastery and find his father's killer. A prisoner of the monks, Fat Yu, assists him along with a drunken monk and helpful nun. To leave the monastery, Dummy must pass the notorious wooden men, robot kung fu machines that test a potential monk's fighting skills. Fat Yu escapes and proves to be a vicious ex-Shaolin crime boss with a sideline in killing families. Dummy must eventually face his destiny, learn the secret arts from a blind hermit and confront his father's killer.

Comment: Jackie's second film for Lo Wei is an unintentional hoot from start to finish. Devoid of dialogue for most of the running time, Jackie's character is treated without any respect by anyone. His mentors are a drunk monk with remarkable bending abilities, a pacifist nun and the evil Fat Yu, imprisoned by the monks but tended by our hero. When Fat Yu escapes, he develops the deadly Lion's Roar technique and a menacing laugh. Under his influence, our mute hero has made many mistakes including the passing of information to the sinister 'Crippled Chemist,' and must now train under a more suitable mentor. The styles used in the film are traditional animal techniques and very formalised. It is only when Jackie employs tumbling to break the rigorous choreography that the film flows. But what, you may ask, about the titular Wooden Men? They are the final test to becoming a proper Shaolin monk, corridors lined with remorseless kung fu robots, kept in place by huge chains. Many a monk has fallen foul and even died at the hands of these emotionless, ruthless machines of death. The only thing is they all look like Bertie Bassett and swing around like drunken puppets. Add the suitably brutal (but strangely funny) sepia flashbacks involving Dummy's dad's killer with a bag on his head, recognisable only by his unusual fighting technique and you've got a jolly bad film. Fun though.

Film Rating: ✪✪✪

Chan Rating: ✪

Killer Meteors (1977)

Director: Lo Wei

Cast: Jackie Chan, Jimmy Wang Yu, Kao Fei, Yu Lin Lung

Plot: Immortal Meteor (Jackie) demands tithe from local villagers or they face the wrath of his mighty weapon. But Killer Weapon, a righteous man, has a Meteor Sword that is capable of defeating him. Throw in some poison, a few assassination plots, double crossing and a stolen pearl that grants ominous premonition and who is to say who will survive?

Comment: Jimmy Wang Yu had been instrumental in the international recognition of the kung fu film, starring in the classic *One Armed* series of films that paved the way for Bruce Lee's assault on the Western market. He would have a great deal of influence on Jackie's future career, but at the time his personal popularity was beginning to decline. Lo Wei decided to place Jimmy opposite Jackie, with Jackie playing the baddie. Later the film would be released in some territories as *Jackie Chan vs. Wang Yu* to capitalise on this 'epic clash of fists and feet.' Sadly, epic is not the term. Lo Wei's dogmatic insistence that everything is played straight is clearly at odds with the ludicrous meteor effects and sub-standard fantasy tree blasting. Somehow Jackie laughing demonically has the opposite of the intended effect - the audience laugh back. Worse still is a multi-threaded plot that seems to have been made up on the spot. Whilst not as torturous as the insane *To Kill With Intrigue*, it still leaves you befuddled. The final encounter between Wang Yu and Chan is passable and violent, set on sticks above a bladed pit, but by then you don't care. Worth a couple of camp laughs but not much more.

Film Rating: ✪✪

Chan Rating: ✪

To Kill With Intrigue (1977)

Director: Lo Wei

Cast: Jackie Chan, Chu Feng, George Wang

Plot: Chau Lee (Jackie) splits with his pregnant girlfriend Chin Chin, secretly entrusting his friend Chin Cheung with her safety, before disrupting his father's birthday party. Fifteen years previously his father had killed most of the Killer Bee Gang, but they return to brutally murder him and his wife in a supernatural assault. Chau Lee must avenge their deaths, then convince his distraught girlfriend that he's alive and not a complete cad. If that were not enough, there's confusion with the Dragon Gang and the Bloody Rain Gang and some gut-wrenching training to contend with. Tough call.

Comment: Further humiliations are bestowed upon Jackie as he is forced to wear a decidedly unconvincing long haired wig, a pair of eyebrows that make him look like Mr Spock, and natty billowing white costume. The most interesting feature of this film is your attitude to Jackie himself – initially you think he's the bad guy because he treats his pregnant girlfriend like dirt and abuses the guests at his father's party. Only as the narrative progresses does it become clear that he is doing this for a reason – to save those he loves. This premise could make for interesting viewing but unfortunately it seems to have happened to every other character too. By the time you have reached the closing showdown you haven't got the foggiest idea who on earth anyone is and whether they're good, evil, dead or alive. In a film like Tsui Hark's *The Butterfly Murders* (1979) this double crossing leads to intrigue and shock revelation, but in *To Kill With Intrigue* you really don't care.

Additional burdens are placed on Chau Lee's shoulders as he has to work up the martial arts prowess to defeat his foes. Normally the teachers in kung fu films look like they are going to scar or cripple their students, but don't. However this is 'high concept tragedy' and hell hath no fury like a woman scarred, so every time Jackie fails to win, he ends up punished – swallowing burning coal or having his face hideously burnt.

Jackie manages to pull a really cracking spear and stick fight that livens matters for a couple of minutes - apparently Lo Wei was asleep while this scene was being shot! Really! *To Kill With Intrigue* is a bizarre and unsatisfying blend of camp and violence that has moments of interest but basically isn't worth the trouble.

Film Rating: ✪✪
Chan Rating: ✪

Despair was beginning to set in at the Lo Wei camp. Jackie had failed to have an effect on the box office so Lo let him film a project with director Chen Chi-Hwa. Chen had directed the better Lo Wei productions with Jackie, giving the star an opportunity to try different styles and techniques. Later on, Jackie would find work for Chen as assistant director on many of his best films including *Police Story*, *Project A* and *Miracles*.

Snake And Crane Arts Of Shaolin (1978)

Director: Chen Chi-Hwa

Cast: Jackie Chan, Nora Miao, Kam Kan

Plot: The eight Shaolin Masters develop the invincible martial art combination of snake and crane styles, writing their findings in a book. They impart the symbol of authority on a spear before mysteriously disappearing. Years later, Su Yin Fong (Jackie) appears in town, in possession of the book. Naturally the multitude of local clans want it, but Yin Fong doesn't let them and beats all comers with his superior techniques. With all this attention, a big showdown is inevitable…

Comment: Although remaining strictly traditional, *Snake And Crane Arts* does offer a fair amount of invention and a phenomenal number of brawls. Chief problem for the viewer is the plethora of clans all fighting to get the book from Su Yin Fong – if they just attacked our hero that would be fine but instead they insist on in-fighting as well. There's the Black Tiger Clan with its bolshy spokeswoman Hung Chu, the Black Dragon Clan with their sneaky sword-wielding infiltrators, and Seng Chu the famous fighter, who dresses like Santa Claus but says "Ha ha ha" instead of "Ho ho ho." The Smelly Beggars Clan make a pongy appearance, as does the always popular Wu Tang Clan and the shorter named Tang Clan with their foxy leader who's willing to bed Su for the book.

If you want unadulterated martial arts scuffles then you've come to the right place. Su Yin Fong is a formidable fighter. The first time we see Jackie's powerful style is when the Ting brothers attack him while he's fishing. The next time he thrashes the Wu Tang Clan in a bar. His confidence is frightening – he goads the clans with the book, and how he knows the fate of the eight masters. High on the impressive list of brawls is a virtuoso spear performance that is a joy to watch – fighting against three mysterious guys in funny hats. Jackie mixes the formalism of his Peking Opera training with an intuitive eye for the filmic fight and the results are stunning. In the end though, it takes balls to defeat them…

Despite being a competent and exciting film, full of action and invention, *Snake And Crane Arts Of Shaolin* did wretched business. Not for the first time Jackie was doubting whether he could hack it as an actor, contemplating resignation once more. It seemed as though even when he made a film that wasn't bad, the audiences just didn't respond.

Film Rating: ✪✪✪
Chan Rating: ✪✪

Half A Loaf Of Kung Fu (1978)

Director: Chen Chi-Hwa

Cast: Jackie Chan, Nora Miao, Kam Kan, James Tien

Plot: Chang To (Jackie) is a kid after a job. He assumes the identity of the Whip Hero, but nobody's fooled as his kung fu is so inept. He eventually gets the chance to deliver some pearls to Fong Wei who also needs help transporting The Soul Pill and The Evergreen Jade. Naturally, such important life-extending artefacts generate attention in the shape of three rival clans. The stage is set for a big rumble. But are Chang To's kung fu skills up to the task or does he need help?

Comment: Lo let the actor and director go off and do their own thing, disgusted by the returns on Jackie's first films. Enthusiastic and ready to try something different, the two decided to ditch the sombre tone of kung fu films and instead attempted to create a pastiche of the genre. Chan's first chance at producing kung fu comedy was met with disbelief by his producer who said that the film was not funny and a waste of celluloid. He only released it after Jackie's later success when it was vilified as a ground-breaking film - something Lo's comedies never were.

Half A Loaf Of Kung Fu has a reputation that precedes it – quick and cheap, it contains the first shoots of Jackie's comic persona, bursting to be released. It is regarded as being formative and inspired – a portent of future greatness. Sadly, when faced with the evidence, you are more likely to favour Lo Wei's opinion, although it is not an unmitigated disaster and there are some moments to enjoy. The title sequence is great - Jackie getting pasted by all and sundry but filmed in an experimental style, all abstract shapes and altered camera speeds to give a sense of humour rather than machismo. The final shot of Jackie practising with his punch post is given a subversive swing by it being knee height! He also includes a Popeye-inspired dream sequence.

The best section is the final gathering of the clans where Jackie gets to do some tree stunts and a very painful bottom-in-the-boiling-pot routine. The real highlight is when Jackie has to defeat the manic Poison Clan leader, despite his limited martial arts knowledge. Our hero has to learn from a variety of manuals that are strewn on the ground – thus he gets thrown a huge distance, runs for a manual, reads it and tries the newly learnt technique. At one point he yanks off his opponent's hair and treats it like a set of nunchuku.

Half A Loaf Of Kung Fu is an accomplished, imaginative and inventive affair. The title sequence alone has loads of ideas and the cast are clearly enjoying themselves. The problem is that the film is far too long with a dull centre hour to sit through. In the cold light of day you will probably laugh more at the inferior *Spiritual Kung Fu*, but not in the way its director intended.

Film Rating: ✪
Chan Rating: ✪✪✪

Magnificent Bodyguards (1978)

Director: Lo Wei

Cast: Jackie Chan, James Tien, 'Bruce' Leung Siu Lung

Plot: Hired to escort a rich family and their sick brother through the notoriously bandit-ridden Stormy Hills, Jackie faces a variety of dangerous encounters before coming face-to-face with the King of the Bandits. But is the King as regal as his name suggests, and how sick is the brother?

Comment: Lo Wei's penchant for trite fist-into-camera shots is given unbridled reign in this messy film. The reason becomes clear when you realise that *Magnificent Bodyguards* was originally shot in 3-D, a rarely well-executed format that is characterised by people throwing things at the camera to make the audience duck. However, even the assistance of headache inducing spectacles can't redeem the film, which basically consists of Jackie's entourage running away from assorted bandits, monks and natives. The restrictions of the film format render most of the fight scenes unfathomable, but there is the odd moment that shines. Jackie's use of monastery bells to defeat a particularly ferocious bunch of adversaries is endearingly awful - "None of them could survive my bells!" he yells triumphantly. Nice costumes though.

Film Rating: ✪
Chan Rating: ✪

Spiritual Kung Fu (aka Karate Ghost Buster) (1978)

Director: Lo Wei

Cast: Jackie Chan, James Tien

Plot: A Ninja steals the Seven Fists instruction manual from a Shaolin temple, a style that can only be defeated by the Five Fists technique. Unfortunately the manual for this is lost. It's down to Yie Lung (Jackie) to learn the style from five master ghosts and apprehend the robber, Yuk San, who is getting stronger every day.

Comment: Unamused by *Half A Loaf Of Kung Fu*, Lo decided to show his still unsuccessful star how to make real comedy – Wei style. Casting the young actor opposite a team of ghosts proved to be a time intensive process as all the multiple exposures had to be executed on cue and in camera. While the results are fairly crude, the effects sequences are competently choreographed. So, technically, this is one of Lo Wei's better and most innovative films.

This is meant to be a comedy but alas isn't that funny. However, mirthful moments include Jackie trying to master calligraphy with an outsized brush, his yearning for dog-meat in the stew and sticking eels down his trousers. And then there's the ghosts. These are particularly unusual ghosts with their white androgyny topped off with shocking red hair. Being invisible, they like nothing better than to fart in people's faces, steal Jackie's trousers and generally misbehave. Jackie's affinity with them is confirmed when he urinates on them. This sort of thing takes up a lot of the running time.

Sophistication is not this film's strong card. It's cheap and crude and the comedy elements are kindest described as broad. Not a total disaster, there are a couple of scenes worth your attention.

Film Rating: ✪✪✪
Chan Rating: ✪

Dragon Fist (1978)

Director: Lo Wei

Cast: Jackie Chan, Nora Miao, James Tien

Plot: The Tang Shan School is disrupted by Lord Chung, its Sifu killed and school signs smashed. How-Yuen (Jackie) perfects the Dragon Fist style so that he can defeat Chung's Flying Kicks and avenge his master. Confronting Lord Chung with his ex-Sifu's daughter and wife, it appears that the old man is riddled with remorse, has cut off his own leg and offers them a gold replacement sign. How-Yuen still seeks revenge though and teams up with local mobster Wei, spurred on by Wei's possession of a remedy for Sifu's widow's illness.

Comment: Jackie's final complete film under the auspices of Lo Wei is a strange affair. Despite the complexity of the plot, the film remains coherent, unfolding as a tragedy where no-one survives unscathed. Wei's inept shooting style and repeated motifs from his other films (the school sign getting shattered in mid air again, crass straight-to-camera slaps and horrible colour matching) can do little to diminish a cracking story that is well acted, if a little melodramatic. As head of the Patience Clan, Lord Chung subverts wonderfully the limbless avenger role while How-Yuen's frustration at Chung's remorse makes for great divided loyalties - you know How-Yuen is going to turn out good in the end but watching his decline due to misunderstanding and treachery is compelling. Even Frankie Chan's occasionally overpowering score makes the film seem a more quality product. There is inevitably a caveat to all this. Intrinsic to the kung fu genre is kung fu, and *Dragon Fist* is remorselessly pedestrian and unimaginative in the fight department.

Film Rating: ✪✪✪
Chan Rating: ✪✪

Lo Wei was losing both money and patience, so when the opportunity came for him to make money from Jackie without the strain of making a film himself, he leapt at the chance. Chan was to star in a two-picture deal with Ng See Yuen's Seasonal Films with debut director Yuen Woo-Ping. Yuen Woo-Ping would become one of the best traditional style martial arts directors and choreographers, making such classics as *Buddhist Fist* (1980) and the remarkable *Tiger Cage II* (1990). He is now well-known in the West for teaching Keanu Reeves kung fu for the smash science fiction film *The Matrix* (1999).

Snake In The Eagle's Shadow (1979)

Director: Yuen Woo-Ping

Cast: Jackie Chan, Hwang Jang Lee, Yuen Siu Tin, Dean Shek

Plot: Chung Chen, Eagle Claw practitioner, is the killer of Snake Fister Pi Chan-Cheng. Chin Fu (Jackie) is a tragic martial arts class whipping-boy who meets eccentric beggar Chow Chi-Chi, who secretly teaches him kung fu. Trouble brews for the school as the pupils are not impressed by their Sifu's lacklustre Dragon and Tiger techniques, but of more concern are the sinister and violent group of people after the elusive Chow.

Comment: The key casting decision was for the Sifu character Chow Chi-Chi, who had to be both adept and comical if the film was to succeed. After a long search he came in the shape of Yuen Siu Tin, Woo Ping's father, a veteran of the original Wong Fei Hung (more on him later) film series, and a long standing actor for Shaw Brothers. Korean kickboxer Hwang Jang Lee was employed to play the evil Eagle style practitioner. With its combination of slapstick comedy and energetic fighting, the film became a big hit, winning new audiences to the kung fu genre without alienating aficionados.

When Chin Fu first sees the old beggar in action he can only marvel at his dexterity. The underdog and beggar then team up in a beautifully choreographed fight of class daftness. Chin Fu's training begins with cryptic messages and handy footprints printed on the courtyard, like those dancing footstep charts popular in the 1950s. His new-found teacher then tortures him mercilessly in the pursuit of snake style excellence. Our hero has to remain painfully upright over lighted incense, perform press-ups between chairs with Sifu sitting on him, and master the slippery snake egg grabbing manoeuvre from a selection of bamboo poles. All of this is under the watchful gaze of Chin Fu's only other real friend, his cat named The Cat. What The Cat lacks in name, he gains in his unique position as second Sifu…

Chin Fu is now set for the final series of fights - the worst involves Hwang Jang Lee facing Jackie in a no-holds barred showdown. The combination of formal and artistic martial arts make for a heady cocktail. We are convinced, however, that the match would have gone the other way if it were not for The Cat.

Snake In The Eagle's Shadow was Jackie's first starring hit and is a joy to watch. Moving away from the stylisation of the traditional kung fu movie, but retaining its choreographed invention, you'll wince as much as laugh. Jackie employs movements that look good rather than being accurate, and develops cod fighting styles that manage the fine balance between realism and farce.

Injury: Hwang Jang Lee's reputation as a formidable fighter was justified as Jackie ended the film minus a tooth-cap.

Film Rating: ✪✪✪
Chan Rating: ✪✪✪

Drunken Master (1979)

Director: Yuen Woo-Ping

Cast: Jackie Chan, Hwang Jang Lee, Yuen Siu Tin, Dean Shek

Plot: Thunderfoot, a hired killer with the deadly Hell's Feet technique, is at large. At Master Wong's school the teacher instructs five animal styles to his pupils, including the mischievous Wong Fei Hung (Jackie). Wong's father, unimpressed with his delinquent ways, decides to let San Sei, a notoriously tough master, teach and discipline the boy. In the meantime, young Fei Hung has found an ally in the shape of an alcoholic kung fu master, unaware that he is San. Events escalate as the King of Sticks threatens the old Sifu and tries to buy Mr Wong's land to mine for coal. If the King of Sticks proves to be no match, maybe he knows a hired killer who will be…

Comment: *Drunken Master* built on the success of *Snake In The Eagle's Shadow* by accentuating the humour of the Sifu character while developing Jackie's burgeoning comedy persona. The real box office winner though, was the decision to cast the new star as Wong Fei Hung, a popular Chinese folk hero from the turn of the century. He had been portrayed in almost 100 films by actor Kwan Tak Hing, and had become a cinematic institution. Having Jackie play such a revered icon was a risk, but by portraying Wong Fei Hung in his formative years they avoided encroachment on the old classics. The inclusion of Yuen Siu Tin helped reinforce the film as did the adoption of the 'Wong Fei Hung Theme,' a stirring, patriotic and catchy tune that is synonymous with him.

Despite being ostensibly the same as *Snake In The Eagle's Shadow*, *Drunken Master* improves on the template by treating Jackie's character as a well-meaning, intelligent mischief maker. He is undisciplined and fights with both his teacher and his own Auntie. There are two major training sessions to enjoy – the first is purely comical with his teacher watching over him, asking him to maintain the painful horse stance

31

over some smouldering incense. He receives aid, temporarily, from a conveniently shaped bench but is discovered and the consequences are truly painful. The lessons with San Sei include bamboo wrist press ups and hanging upside down whilst filling buckets of water using teacups. Any hopes of Wong Fei Hung escaping this torture is thwarted by his canny master's trapped house and the string tied around his toe.

Key to the film is alcohol. The drunken master's astonishing range of dodges, parries and nonchalant side punches are fuelled by his drink intake. What Fei Hung needs is to learn the Eight Drunken Gods Style, which he does, suitably soused. He's not keen on the Wanton Woman style though - it's a man thing you see. Hwang Jang Lee again plays the super villain, and the more fluid and original showdown surpasses that of the previous film.

Drunken Master deservedly established Jackie Chan as the star to watch. To see him fighting someone but pausing every once in a while to poke his attacker's comrade in alternate eyes symbolises the film in a single shot – funny, violent and assured. From now on Hong Kong would have a new star. Only one problem – his two picture deal with Seasonal was over and the stifling world of Lo Wei beckoned back. This time Lo would not be lending out his big star, despite the fact it was not he who got Jackie to the top.

Injury: Concussed by Hwang Jang Lee, Jackie also sustained a cut to the eye - the scar is still visible.

Film Rating: ✪✪✪✪

Chan Rating: ✪✪✪✪

Jackie was itching to direct his own picture - his way. Lo Wei was fast losing his grip on the young star and agreed to allow him the freedom - his current form should result in a tidy profit, so why not? The results gave Lo Wei substantial returns, but emphasised his need to hold onto Jackie, whatever the cost.

Fearless Hyena (1979)

Director: Jackie Chan

Cast: Jackie Chan, James Tien, Shih Tien, Li Kuan, Yen Shi-kwan

Plot: Yen and three cloaked assassins want Chen (Chan) dead. Jackie's grandfather warns him not to teach anyone kung fu, but Jackie gets a head teacher's position at a martial arts school. Recognising the kung fu style of Chen, Yen finds Jackie's grandfather and kills him. It's time for revenge.

Comment: For a debut, *Fearless Hyena* is assured and innovative but still lacks the confidence to push away from the traditional kung fu picture. Often considered the first part of Chan's 'Pastoral Trilogy' (the others being *Young Master* and *Dragon Lord*) the three films provide a bridge between the Chan of the 70s and the superstar of the 80s. Jackie's genius was to break from kung fu comedy (a genre in which he was not the first but still a pioneer) into comedy that included kung fu. Key to the otherwise horribly derivative showdown is Jackie's adoption of 'Emotional Style' kung fu, in which he play-acts extreme emotional states to beat up his opponent.

Further developing the lazy persona that would run to *Dragon Lord*, our hero goes to extraordinary lengths to do nothing! Naturally he'd rather be a pampered, well paid, teacher at a local martial arts school than an undertaker's assistant, especially when the undertaker has an unhealthy love of his own coffins. Our scamp of a hero is more likely to disarm his opponent by tickling them, a mirror of Yen's pinching technique, than conventional kung fu. The real highlight involves the series of comedic kung fu challenges to the school in which Jackie adopts a number of increasingly cunning disguises. His most audacious is an alternately wanton and coy girl who befuddles her sex-mad opponent, before bashing him around with her ample but errant breasts! Not that the finale is a let down - when facing the three sword bearing Ninja our hero dodges their blades by millimetres. How do we know? You can see, in slow motion, the swords cutting off tufts of hair.

Fearless Hyena is flawed but fun and there's never a dull moment. Jackie's fighting styles perfectly parody the traditional animal forms, yet remain convincing throughout.

Film Rating: ✪✪✪
Chan Rating: ✪✪✪

Fearless Hyena was a huge success and the studios started taking great interest in this new star. Eager to get on with a new, and well-paid contract elsewhere, Jackie was brought down to earth with a resounding crunch. Golden Harvest, run by Raymond Chow and Leonard Ho, offered him millions of dollars to join them, but he was still contractually bound to Lo Wei.

Fearless Hyena II (1980)

Director: Lo Wei

Cast: Jackie Chan, James Tien, Shih Tien

Plot: There is none.

Comment: In the light of the original's success, it was off to Taiwan to shoot a sequel. Lo himself returned to the director's chair. Jackie lasted two days before he could take no more. Lo's wife made a plea for the downhearted star to return, but ultimately this was where the two parted.

After two days of filming the average director would admit defeat at the loss of their lead, or reshoot the film from scratch, but Lo knew he could exploit Jackie's new-found star presence and the film has been circulated ever since as a Jackie Chan film. To make up for the missing stock, Lo reworked the film to include a Chan-a-like with the incredible ability to look nothing like Chan, and some jarring subplots that make no narrative sense. To show that there were no hard feelings between director and ex-star, Lo Wei thoughtfully added some snide dialogue including derogatory comments about the size of our hero's proboscis ("That big nosed b*****d"). Even Lo Wei's back catalogue is plundered without any regard to stock or character matching - the feeling of deja vu is strong as you 'enjoy' again the rib tickling 'eel down the trousers' routine from *Spiritual Kung Fu* or marvel at the climax shots from the original *Fearless Hyena*.

Bad films fall neatly into two categories - those that are so bad that they are fun (c.f. *Fantasy Mission Force*) and those that are just bad. *Fearless Hyena II* falls squarely into the latter category - it makes no sense, is poorly acted and the action is dull. Avoid like the plague.

Film Rating: ✪

Chan Rating: ✪

4: Reaping The Golden Harvest

Away from creative and financial constraints, Jackie was given free reign at Golden Harvest to direct his second feature. Behind the scenes though, things were not good. There was the severance contract with Lo Wei to settle, a matter not helped by his alleged altering of the document. Secondly, there were the Triads to contend with, all eager to get a slice of the Jackie pie. Problem one needed cash and lawyers, something Raymond Chow had in numbers. Problem two needed a go-between – Jimmy Wang Yu. Negotiations were long and dangerous but Jimmy sorted the problem at great personal risk.

The Young Master (1980)

Director: Jackie Chan

Starring: Yuen Biao, Shih Tien, Lily Lee

Plot: At the lion dance competition Dragon (Jackie) is defeated by Tiger, a brotherly classmate, who has taken a bribe from the rival school to be the head of their lion. Sifu Tien is not happy and Tiger leaves the school. Wai Yee, head of the rival gym, recruits Tiger and gets him to rescue a long-haired psychopath using his fan skills, before setting him up at a bank job. Dragon is suspected of being one of the evil team, as he too uses a fan. He is pursued by the police chief Sang Kung and his bench wielding son (Yuen Biao). It is down to Dragon to return Tiger to the school and take on the psycho with the evil laugh.

Comment: Jackie was given carte blanche at Golden Harvest and it shows! The opening lion dance is a joy to watch - two people per lion, eating vegetables out of wooden buckets whilst balancing precariously on them. Our hero then discovers Tiger has betrayed the school but is unwilling to defeat him - the resulting dextrous encounter has the trophy shuttlecock kicked from person to person, on a plank high above the ground, while still maintaining the character of the lions. It was on *Young Master* that Chan's reputation as a perfectionist was first mooted - in the fan scene, one shot alone took over 1000 takes to satisfy his standards. Jackie's plan for the film was to create the ultimate, traditional, martial arts film with the humorous edge that made him his reputation. From this aspect *Young Master* is a roaring success. When attacked by police at a Buddhist temple he dodges swords with millimetres to spare, whilst managing to convince one that atheism is not a wise stance! Additional fun is had with Sang Kong and his son, a deranged bench wielder played by Yuen Biao. Jackie's capture by the pair who think he's the dreaded White Fan, leads to a variety of escape attempts, including climbing between two buildings. A fight with Sang Kong has Dragon defending himself because he scared a goldfish to death!

On release, *Young Master* was a phenomenal smash, breaking all box office records in Hong Kong and justifying Raymond Chow's enormous investment. Today, it still holds as an exhilarating example of the genre but does suffer a problem in that the showdown lasts for over twenty minutes. It's impressive and funny, but Jackie's reliance on traditional side-on, long take kung fu is at odds with the rest of the film. That said, *Young Master* is a landmark in his career and a real pointer for what was to come.

Injury: Broken Nose
Film Rating: ✪✪✪
Chan Rating: ✪✪✪

With negotiations going on between Jimmy Wang Yu, Lo Wei, Golden Harvest and the Triads, it was considered wise that Jackie should leave Hong Kong temporarily and try to become a big star in the hard-to-crack US market. The Golden Harvest plan was simple - take their top star to America in a film made by an American director - best of both worlds.

Battle Creek Brawl (aka The Big Brawl) (1980)
Director: Robert Clouse, Cast: Jackie Chan, Mako, Kristine De Bell, Jose Ferrer

Plot: The 1930s. Jerry Kwan (Chan) helps at his father's restaurant in America. There is trouble with the protection rackets and naturally Jerry tries to sort it out. His antics catch the eye of a local gang boss who wants to use Jerry's unique fighting skills in the Battle Creek Brawl contest. Jerry declines but the evil Dominici kidnaps Jerry's wholesome sister-in-law-to-be so he is forced to enter the contest - facing both the contestants and the local mob.

Comment: Robert Clouse, who had made Bruce Lee's last completed film *Enter The Dragon*, was the director on this one. The main problem was that Jackie Chan was not Bruce Lee and *Enter The Dragon* was Lee's least impressive film. Chan did not enjoy his experience - his English was still developing, the shoot went on for ever and, worse still, the fights were choreographed by someone else. Someone very slow.

Despite the wholly negative press that *Battle Creek Brawl* has received over the years, it is actually not that bad. It's not good either but there are some reasons to watch, even if they are the wrong ones! The best sequence occurs right at the start of the film when Jerry faces three hoods. Despite demands that he shouldn't fight, he manages to take out all three of them by falling over, and using accidental kicks with surreptitious punches disguised as flailing gestures. After this, the film goes seriously downhill. At one point Jerry is involved in a roller-skating race which is like a bizarre hybrid of *The Sting* (1973), *Rollerball* (1975) and *Saturday Night Fever* (1977). The film is set in the 1930s so it comes as some shock seeing Jackie in a yellow jump-suit and one of his opponents wearing a gold spandex disco suit! The overall result is sporadically amusing but the main problem is the pace. Jackie has complained that he could get three punches in before the opponent even blocked the first one, but really he underestimated - seven looks more appropriate! *Battle Creek Brawl*, unsurprisingly, did not lead to stardom in the states.

Film Rating: ✪✪
Chan Rating: ✪✪

Cannonball Run (1981)

Director: Hal Needham

Cast: Jackie Chan, Burt Reynolds, Farrah Fawcett, Michael Hui, Sammy Davies Jr, Peter Fonda

Plot: The Cannonball Run is a driving contest from Connecticut to California with a fortune at stake. Only thing is, it's illegal. Our group of intrepid drivers from all over the world will bump, speed and cheat to ensure a win.

Comment: Golden Harvest figured that perhaps America needed a gradual introduction to Jackie so rather than cast him as star, they set about looking for an alternative. *Cannonball Run* was a multi-star picture, so much so that Chan is just one of a multitude of poorly-defined incidental characters. To add insult to injury, Jackie and actor Michael Hui (a hugely popular comedian in Hong Kong due to his Mr Boo character) were cast as Japanese drivers without any real purpose other than to provide cheap racial gags. The only time Jackie even steps out of the car is to beat up some bikers, which included Peter Fonda. There's a reasonable double kick, but the filmmakers seemed to have wanted Bruce Lee or Sonny Chiba. A poor film when it came out and even worse in retrospect, *Cannonball Run* was highly successful in the US.

Injury: Only his pride.
Film Rating: ✪
Chan Rating: ✪

The terrible time Jackie had regarding Lo Wei's contract was resolved so he returned to Hong Kong to resume his career. With a free reign from Raymond Chow, Jackie had full responsibility for producing his 'welcome home' picture, originally entitled *Young Master In Love* to capitalise on his last big success, but later changed to *Dragon Lord*. With an unprecedented budget and a shooting time that took up a year, *Dragon Lord* was monumental in execution.

Dragon Lord (1982)

Director: Jackie Chan

Cast: Jackie Chan, Mars, Chen Hui-Min, Sidney Yim, Whang In-Sik

Plot: Our hero Dragon, is the son of a local merchant and pretty good when it comes to sports. He also thinks he's a bit of a ladies' man, deciding to reveal his affections to his chosen love by way of a letter attached to a balloon. Sadly, the balloon flies the wrong way and young Dragon, in a frantic effort to retrieve it, catches wind of a devious plot to sell off China's national treasures. Can Dragon manage to defeat the bad guys, win the local shuttlecock game, get the treasure back and win the girl? What do you think?

Comment: Jackie is all too ready to dismiss *Dragon Lord* as an expensive mess, but he should really watch the film again - it's great. The opening scene alone is worth the price of admission as we see four teams compete to get a ball into their squad's coloured bag. Simple? Well the ball is at the top of a rickety wooden pyramid. Cue lots of falling bodies, trampled hands and a toppling mass of people that looks exceedingly painful, culminating in a cheeky win for Dragon. Exhilarating stuff. Jackie's perfectionist approach to film-making became apparent - he claims they got through 2,900 shots in this sequence. The other sports match is pretty special too, a kick shuttlecock match that is dazzling in its execution. He doesn't let go in the fight scenes either - a punch up at a flour mill has Chan swinging on ladders, balancing precariously on ledges and, in a single take, falling from a beam and crashing onto his friend below.

Key to much of Chan's best work is the balance between comedy and danger, perfectly illustrated when he is spotted and attacked on the bad guys' roof. From his tippy-toe attempts to retrieve the balloon, to his subsequent endeavours to dodge spears thrust through the slates, Chan's elastic features show true mastery of the form. But it's not just the bad guys that Dragon fears. His father expects him to study all the Chinese arts, resulting in an insane poetry recital with Dragon taking directions from sneaky crib sheets hidden around the room, and frantically miming servants.

Even if it is a little uneven, this is an unfairly overlooked film. It is also the first time Jackie used out-takes at the end of the movie to show the filming process, and all too often how it goes wrong! Nowadays, no one ever leaves a Jackie Chan film before the credits have finished. Not if they have any sense that is.

Injury: No one fell from the pyramid unscathed, Jackie included.
Film Rating: ✪✪✪✪
Chan Rating: ✪✪✪✪

Fantasy Mission Force (1982)

Director: Chu Yen Ping

Cast: Jackie Chan, Brigitte Lin Ching-Hsia, Jimmy Wang Yu, Chang Ling, Sun Yuen

Plot: The world's four top generals have been kidnapped by the Japanese. The rescue mission, with the promise of cash rewards, is given to a band of assorted criminals and misfits. They have four days to prevent a world morale crisis.

Comment: Remember Jimmy Wang Yu, the guy who saved Jackie's butt over the Lo Wei hassles? Well this was Jackie's first chance to return the favour, appearing in this Taiwanese production in a recurring cameo role.

Insane is not a strong enough term to describe *Fantasy Mission Force*. It is quite simply the most bizarre film you are likely to see. Two of the main characters are renegades from an Asian/Scot army camp (camp, incidentally, being the operative term for the whole piece) one of whom wears a leotard with his kilt, a prickly pom-pom on a chain and spiked Kaiser helmet. Another is a beggar thief with a line in food-eating songs. And yet another is a white-suited mercenary with an irate leather-clad bazooka-toting girlfriend called Lili. This in itself would make for strange viewing but you ain't seen nothing yet.

When we first meet our Asian/Scot friends they are in fast motion

Benny Hill mode complete with theme music and slappy baldy gags. They encounter a tribe of leopardskin-clad Amazonian women with paper bags on their heads. This is disconcerting because it's a while before you realise they are women, bulging biceps and ferocious fighting abound until the bags are removed and – like magic – they shed pounds, grow breasts and look shapely! Not content with tying our heroes up with flying scarves, they further humiliate the group by forcing the men to wear saucy seaside postcard boards around their necks and boil two of them up for dinner. A later encounter in a haunted house has the group terrorised by hopping vampires, ancient gamblers and disembodied hands waving toilet paper.

Jackie drifts in and out of the film seemingly at random. We first see him attempting to fix a wrestling match, his garland-coated sedan reaching waist height so that he walks with it! He participates in a smoking contest, then later saves Lili from the Amazonian women, armed with a runaway chicken. His final appearance is at the film's dramatic close where, apart from machine-gunning about a hundred neo-Nazis and getting to grips with a high recoil garden rake, he faces the double-crossing Jimmy Wang Yu. Surprisingly, this fight is rather good - Jackie jumping out of cars seconds before they are hit by evil Jimmy's bulldozer, dodging his flexi-sword while jumping from roof to roof.

Total utter madness, there's atrocious make-up, minstrels, musical numbers, decapitations, crucifixion, bottom exposure, a Nazi torch procession and an Amazon Queen who dresses like Caligula and bounds across water. *Fantasy Mission Force* demands viewing, preferably with friends, preferably drunk. This is appalling, but it is so much fun to watch. Check out the longer Chinese version for added mirth and stupidity.

Film Rating: ✪✪✪✪✪ or ✪ depending on whether or not you have a warped sense of humour

Chan Rating: ✪

Ignoring any concepts of shame or taste, the producers of *Fire Dragon* rearranged new footage with segments of *Fantasy Mission Force* to make a whole new film. By dubbing the actors and replacing some with stand-ins, they weave a different tale out of the same thread. Ineptly. Jackie 'plays' Alan and the heroes try to enlist his help. How do we know it's Alan? Well, we never see more than the back of his head and, to emphasise who he is, his room is covered with Jackie Chan posters. Shameless. Please note that this sort of thing happens quite a lot. You really do have to be careful about what you buy. *Master Of Disaster* 'starring' Jackie Chan and Moon Lee, is another shameless exercise that rejigs material from other Chan films.

Winners And Sinners (aka Five Lucky Stars) (1983)

Director: Samo Hung

Cast: Jackie Chan, Samo Hung, Richard Ng, Michael Hui, Charlie Chin, John Shum, Stanley Fong, Yuen Biao, Sibelle Hu

Plot: Five men become friends in prison. On release, still suspected by the police, the group become involved with some really bad guys and a pile of counterfeit money. Will their subtle disguise (and new female partner) as the Lucky Stars Cleaning Co let them survive the film and stay outside of gaol?

Comment: Brainchild of Samo Hung, *Winners And Sinners* was the first in a series of ensemble comedies designed to maximise public appeal by gathering together a group of popular comedians into one project. The result was the hugely successful *Lucky Stars* films, named after the cleaning/decorating company formed by our illustrious criminal heroes and matched only by the *Aces Go Places* series that started the year before. Eventually the two would merge for *Lucky Stars Go Places*. Jackie has a supporting role, as a policeman friend of the five.

Jackie's segment allows him the opportunity to put his roller-skating skills learnt in *Battle Creek Brawl* to decent use. It's similar to the famous scene from *Some Mothers Do 'Ave 'Em* with Frank Spencer roller-skating under a lorry - but this is Jackie and it's a whole lot faster and scarier. Not content with having jumped through a flaming hoop on roller-skates in a competition, our hero has to catch the criminals by hanging on the side of several cars before skating under an 18 wheeler! He allows a car to run over him, skates over a Volkswagen Beetle and in a moment of sheer madness, forces a motorcyclist off of his bike and rides off on it!

While worth seeing on the strength of Jackie alone, the rest of the film does not disappoint with its easy-going combination of daft gags, silly faces and bonkers stunts. There's even some great kung fu to enjoy (this is Samo after all), a mad sequence with a forklift truck and Richard Ng's 'Invisible Man' routine. For some reason John Shum's wild-haired political activist is hysterical without him doing anything.

Film Rating: ❂❂❂
Chan Rating: ❂❂

Cannonball Run II (1983)

Director: Hal Needham

Cast: Jackie Chan, Burt Reynolds, Richard Kiel

Plot: Can't you guess? Oh all right then. There's a wacky illegal race in America. Again.

Comment: You would have thought that after the unmitigated disaster that was *Cannonball Run* that Jackie would have stayed well away from this reprehensible sequel. After all, he was big in the East, why be a stooge in the West? Sadly the first film proved to be successful and Jackie was under contract to appear. Michael Hui managed to avoid this one, so they arranged a new partner for Jackie in the shape of Richard Kiel, better known for his role as Jaws in those cheesy James Bond films. Jackie gets to beat up some bikers, again, and knocks a couple of guys out at the 'climax.' The rest of his mercifully limited screen time is involved with computer gadgetry in a Mitsubishi. Reprehensible, sexist, racist and unfunny, we had to sit through this travesty so you don't have to.

Injury: Deflated ego.
Film Rating: ❂
Chan Rating: ❂

5: Twinkle Twinkle Lucky Superstar

After a string of non-personal projects and abortive attempts at other markets, Jackie embarked on *Project A* originally called *Pirate Patrol*, written by long-time collaborator and scriptwriter Edward Tang. It is Chan's first genuine masterpiece, a perfect blend of comedy, excitement, stunts and fighting. It also established a closer on-screen tie between the three brothers of the Opera School: Samo Hung, Jackie and Yuen Biao. The climactic scene, featuring the three flying through the air on the back of an explosion, sums them up perfectly. They all ended up getting hurt.

Project A (1983)

Director: Jackie Chan

Cast: Jackie Chan, Samo Hung, Yuen Biao, Dick Wei

Plot: Hong Kong. The waterways are under the control of the evil pirate Sanpao and the Coast Guard/Navy seem powerless to do anything. Things are not helped by the corrupt Police chief tipping off the pirates and selling them arms, or the running brawls between the Police and the Navy. Following the sabotage of the Navy's remaining ships, Dragon Ma (Chan) and chums are forced to join the Police under young upstart Tsu, but Dragon quits after busting a local gangster, due to interference. He then has to disrupt the arms deal, enlist the help of ex-friend and mah jong player Samo, reform the disengaged Coast Guard and seek out Sanpao.

Comment: *Project A* marks the first successful fusion of Jackie's comedy, mixing the kung fu humour of his earlier films with the sort of loopy megastunts that made the silent comedians so successful. It is pure visual storytelling and goes a long way to explain Jackie's world-wide success. The humour is universal - the same as that of the silent comedians and later Gene Kelly or Jacques Tati. The debt to those is written throughout *Project A* - there is the club arrest scene with bodies tumbling down the stairs like Chaplin's *1am*, the bike sequence is pure Buster Keaton and the mad clock-tower routine is from Harold Lloyd's *Safety Last*. Also, Jackie makes his first real departure from the two staple Hong Kong action genres, the crime caper or the traditional monastery type. This not only gave the film originality, it has also meant that it looks as fresh today as it did in 1983 - it provides a nostalgic air that harks back to both the comedians who provided so much inspiration and to a decadent colonial past that is uniquely Hong Kong.

Top in the humour stakes is a madcap bicycle chase through the back streets. Dragon has already displayed his cycling skills as he can park his own bike 'long range' but this time the bad guys are hot on his trail! The sequence is tightly choreographed with one lunatic encounter leading to another in quick succession. His bravura has to be punished though. After a particularly flashy attack, our hero's bike seat flies off, and he sits on the spike. The bottom clenching results are wonderfully exaggerated. This states another of Jackie's golden rules of comedy – it is always funnier if the good guy gets hurt as well. In the bar room brawl at the start, Dragon and Tsu both hit each other with chairs. Looking each other bravely in the eye they both discretely retreat out of sight to wince in agony! Not that Jackie gets all of the best scenes of course, there are many other great moments - Samo desperately holding onto his winning mah jong hand while a major fight is in progress and a beautifully choreographed Samo & Jackie fight at the tea house.

Project A is also memorable as the film that introduced the 'money shot' stunt - the stunt so stupid or foolhardy that only someone without insurance could possibly do it. In trying to escape the bad guys, Dragon ends up handcuffed to a flagpole. He climbs it and jumps from it, through the skylight of a facing clock tower and ends up dangling from the minute hand of the clock. He falls, rip! through an awning below, rip! through the next one and thwap! right on the ground. All in one take. He had spent a week on initial preparation, trying to get the nerve to do it. It had been pre-tested, as all stunts should, before committing it to take - with a bag of dirt! Not quite the same thing. Somehow Jackie got the nerve, fell, rip! through an awning below, bounce! off the next one and splat! straight to the ground and onto a stretcher. Handcuffed.

The climactic fight between the towering pirate king Sanpao (Dick Wei) and our heroes is awe-inspiring. Sanpao looks like he could kick through walls. When our team get going, the pace is frightening and for one brief moment you even doubt they are going to make it. But hey, it's the three brothers, of course they'll make it. Sanpao's demise at the end of all this violence is a comic staple, but it works to great effect – we won't be seeing him in the sequel!

Project A may not contain Jackie's best individual scenes, fights or stunts, but put together in such a tight little package, the case can be made for this being his most satisfying film. It has all of the elements essential to a great Chan experience - you'll laugh, you'll gasp, you'll cringe. The fights are violent, the comedy hysterical and the script keeps everything together nicely. Classic.

Injury: Injured neck from the clocktower fall. Broken nose.

Film Rating: ✪✪✪✪✪

Chan Rating: ✪✪✪✪✪

Wheels On Meals (aka Spartan X) (1984)

Director: Samo Hung

Cast: Jackie Chan, Yuen Biao, Samo Hung, Lola Forner, Benny 'The Jet' Urquidez

Plot: Yuen and Jackie are Chinese fast food sellers in Barcelona who become involved with a pickpocket prostitute called Sylvia, who unbeknownst to them all, is heiress to Count Lobas' fortune. On their trail is bumbling PI Moby (Samo), and the henchmen of Sylvia's evil half brother, who wants to get his hands on her wealth.

Comment: Hot on the heels of their first major teaming, the dynamic trio launched their next venture, this time with Samo at the helm. Consciously aiming for the international market, they filmed in Barcelona and cast Lola Forner as the lust interest. Also aboard was Benny 'The Jet' Urquidez, an undefeated American kickboxing champion whose pull-no-punches style of martial arts did not go down well with Jackie, who was hit too hard, too many times. It didn't stop a rematch in *Dragons Forever* though…

Surprisingly, the best sequence in the film is the car chase. After the most impressive piece of parallel parking ever, our heroes rescue Sylvia from an attempted kidnap but are pursued by two yellow and black cabs. They dodge and weave their way across Barcelona taking in virtually every landmark in the city, even flying over a busy motorway! Finally they use mustard, ketchup and a variety of restaurant equipment to cause one of the most spectacular car rolls you'll ever see, before accidentally losing Samo down a hill in a horribly frightening fall. Be warned though - great though this sequence is, it does reinforce another motif - the Mitsubishi plug. Jackie's success in Japan is huge and over the years he has had a long and mutually profitable arrangement with Mitsubishi cars. This early example of product placement is as subtle as a brick in the face – even using an old granny to shamelessly extol the virtues of her car!

The climactic castle fight is a genuine classic, beautifully playing on the strengths of the three protagonists before they even get in! Jackie goes for the complicated building climb, Yuen utilises a grapple and rope and Samo uses the front door. This self-deprecating style makes Samo's roguish character all the more likeable. Naturally the showdown is set, each of the three facing their own adversary. Samo gets the Count's son in an East-Vs-West fencing match, while Yuen's incredible tumbling on leather sofas is the acrobatic highlight of the film. Most people recall the encounter with Benny 'The Jet' as the peak of Jackie's fights. Well it is good, very fast and extremely violent, but when the dust has settled there is something missing. The confrontation may be his most realistic and bone-crunching, but it lacks the inventiveness and humour that makes Jackie's fights so special.

Wheels On Meals (the title is such because Golden Harvest had bad returns on two films beginning with 'M' and didn't want to risk a third) was a huge success and even broke the international market as intended. You will undoubtedly get a lot of pleasure from watching it, but deep down the film is lacking. Sylvia's character is incongruous, a matter not helped by a 'tumbling hair moment' complete with crappy music every time she is introduced into a scene. The plot isn't clear until a good two thirds of the way through, the bikers and the randy Italians (in Spain?) are extraneous, and the mental asylum sub-plot tasteless, but sporadically funny. Coherence has never been the foremost reason to watch a Jackie Chan film, but a tighter script could really have helped here.

Injury: Lots of bruises fighting Benny
Film Rating: ✪✪✪
Chan Rating: ✪✪✪

My Lucky Stars (1985)

Director: Samo Hung

Cast: Jackie Chan, Samo Hung, Richard Ng, Sibelle Hu, Charlie Chin, Eric Tsang, Dick Wei, Yuen Biao, Michiko Nishiwaki

Plot: Muscles (Chan) and Ricky (Yuen) chase some Ninja criminals but Ricky is captured. Muscles enlists the help of Kidstuff (Samo) and the other Lucky Stars to infiltrate the Scarecrow Club in Japan, bust the bad cop and rescue all and sundry. A mighty task, but with top cops on the scene what could possibly go wrong?

Comment: The success of *Winners And Sinners* (known as *Five Lucky*

Stars in Japan) meant sequels were inevitable, so the team got together again for more madcap antics. Jackie and Yuen appear once again as policemen in a cameo capacity. After a manic car chase at the start, with Mitsubishis bounding over picket fences, our heroes find themselves at a fairground. They climb a Ferris wheel which is scary, but not as scary as when they get off of it - Yuen doing the most incredible acrobatics while Jackie elects 'just' to jump. Needless to say mayhem ensues. After this, the cops take a backburner while the Lucky Stars get together. This is a bit of a hit-and-miss affair, alternately hysterical and crass with some needlessly extended diarrhoea jokes and the sadistic treatment of Miss Woo at the hands of our randy comedy criminals. But fear not, all is not lost as Jackie comes back and the stage is set for a long and impressive climax. Trails lead to the carnival, and the film takes a surreal turn as Samo and Jackie fight it out in a haunted house and a bizarre upside-down room. Jackie dresses up in a Disney style character costume and fights several swordsmen. The final punch-up is brutal and funny, with Yuen catching the corrupt policeman and Jackie kicking tough guy Dick Wei off of a balcony.

My Lucky Stars at its best, combines high speed, high intensity combat, stunts and jokes – there are more gags in the first half hour than in most Hollywood comedies, and more fights in the last half an hour than most action flicks.

Film Rating: ✪✪✪
Chan Rating: ✪✪

Twinkle, Twinkle Lucky Stars (1985)

Director: Samo Hung

Cast: Jackie Chan, The Lucky Stars, Rosamund Kwan, Yuen Biao

Plot: The Lucky Stars and Ba Wah take a trip to Pattanya and get embroiled in all the usual amounts of (futile) girl chasing, madcap antics and big punch-ups. On the way, their paths occasionally brush with Inspectors Muscles (Jackie) and Fung (Yuen Biao), female sword wielding assassins, bazookas and toxic waste. Normal day at the office then…

Comment: The huge success of the previous films meant a further outing was inevitable. Our Lucky Star friends, as sexually desperate as ever, degenerate to new lows trying to bed the delightful Ba Wah. They even arrange a fake fire to get her in the bath. They also tunnel beneath some unfortunate sunbathers and Sandy (Richard Ng) resorts to black magic. Naturally these plans generally fail with amusing results.

Jackie and Yuen reprise their police officer roles whenever the film needs a bit of an action uplift. This is a Samo film so there's lots of violence that contrasts with comedy – parascenders are gunned out of the sky, Kidstuff and Ba Wah are nearly blown out of their speedboat and then they have to face a horde of sword wielding women. Jackie's entrance involves taking on a motley bunch of thugs at a dockside warehouse. All the usual crew are there and the professionalism shows – it's a bone-crunching mini-manic-masterpiece of flying bodies and shuddering thumps as Samo's regular stunt team take some remarkably painful-looking knocks. Jackie may not be the star of the film but his director sure puts him through the mill. Later on, Muscles is required to perform some serious motorcycle stunts and there are too many explosions for it to be entirely safe. If that were not enough, he gets to fight Richard Norton too! The Marx Brothers/Monty Python-style ending, involving a lift and half the film community of Hong Kong, has to be seen to be believed.

A lot of fun, completely shallow and with no discernible coherence, *Twinkle Twinkle Lucky Stars* is like a pick 'n' mix bag of crude humour and mad violence.

Film Rating: ✪✪✪
Chan Rating: ✪✪

The Protector (1985)

Director: James Glickenhaus

Cast: Jackie Chan, Danny Aiello, Bill Wallace, Moon Lee, Sally Yeh

Plot: Our police heroes' (Danny and Jackie) unorthodox drug busting antics are not appreciated by their superiors. They travel to Hong Kong when the daughter of a tycoon is kidnapped. With tons of lethal hardware between the drug producers and justice, will the dynamic duo (well, dynamic mono and Danny Aiello) make it out alive?

Comment: The completion of *The Protector* would mark the end of Jackie's second stab at the US market but not the end of his involvement with the film. He was so disgruntled with it and his treatment by the American press, that he re-shot key sequences to improve the final product. Jackie had not been impressed by director Glickenhaus's unimaginative use of his abilities - restricting fight scenes to a couple of punches and predominantly featuring him brandishing a firearm and casually cussing. The role was more suited to a pedestrian Western cop than an acrobatic Eastern one. Of further concern to Chan was the casual use of nudity in the production, something he had felt unhappy with since his involvement in *All In The Family*. Thus there are two versions of *The Protector* - the original one and the re-mix directed by Jackie. Naturally we favour the latter although both of them are fairly average films.

Glickenhaus created a film which compensates for his lack of originality with money and hardware - it has all the markings of an 80s Hollywood action film. Typically, it relies on spectacle rather than speed or skill. There are some exciting moments - an early gun fight, a motorbike routine onto a boat and a helicopter crash at the finale - but they could have used any star in the role. Jackie's response was to reshoot key sequences, add Sally Yeh, a gym fight and generally polish the whole affair. While Jackie's version at least has some good fight scenes (in Glickenhaus's version the adversaries hardly touch each other), it is still based upon an inferior story and Robert Clouse's script-by-numbers. That is not to say the film is unwatchable, it's just a waste of talent. But at least it gave Jackie ideas for *Police Story*.

Film Rating: ✪✪
Chan Rating: ✪ or ✪✪✪ (depending on which version you watch)

Heart Of Dragon (aka First Mission) (1985)

Director: Samo Hung

Cast: Jackie Chan, Samo Hung, Dick Wei, Lam Ching-Ying, Emily Chu

Plot: Tad Fung (Jackie) moves from his job in the SWAT team to join the CID, but really he wants to be a sailor. His personal life consists of looking after his 29 year old brother Dodo, who has not developed mentally, and trying to maintain a relationship with his girlfriend Jenny. A jewellery robbery results in gangster Mr Kim wanting his goods back - Dodo unwittingly holding up the escaping thief Fa and hiding the loot with one of his friends. Mr Kim kidnaps Dodo and demands that Tad bring Fa to him. With the help of his old SWAT team friends, Tad must free Fa, rescue his brother and seek revenge...

Comment: Often tagged as 'the Hong Kong *Rain Man*' despite being made before that film, *Heart Of Dragon* is a genuine oddity in Jackie's career and also the one with the most apt title. Partially scripted by Barry Wong, a Samo regular who later penned John Woo's awesome bloodshed films *The Killer* and *Hard Boiled*, this is a tight and believable drama.

Samo plays the cruelly named Dodo, a man whose mental condition leaves him infantile, yet aware of society's need for him to behave like an adult. What could so easily become a mawkish or ridiculous performance is given genuine pathos. Dodo is not a character who is humourless - he is a rounded individual whose actions are affected by his condition, not driven by them. Most of his friends are schoolchildren and he blends in with them well, giving them the irresponsibility of childhood and the protection of a father-sized figure. It leads to disastrous events in a restaurant when he can't pay the ice cream bill. Jackie's performance as Tad is no less remarkable - he has done the honourable thing by looking after his brother at the expense of his own future but has reached his limit. This is no gurney-faced performance. When Tad reflects on what he could have done with his life he transfers the guilt squarely onto Dodo's lap, ceasing to be the sympathetic character we normally associate with Jackie. He is embarrassed by his brother - pointing out their relationship to passers-by when they holds hands, lest they be considered gay. When Dodo tries to find a job and is humiliated by restaurant staff, it is down to friend Yan to bring him home. Even then, Tad is unrepentant - "I'm cold-blooded, so what?" These incredibly uncomfortable scenes are never exploitative but rather close to the bone. When Tad finally realises that he is selfish, the brothers hug and burst into tears in a deep felt outpouring that is hard to watch. Tad accepts his responsibilities and loses his dream, but tragically it is his love for his brother that eventually causes them to be apart anyway. Tad's girlfriend Jenny, initially dubious because everyone indicated that Tad wants a wife to look after Dodo, is ultimately happy to become his guardian - because the reason for Tad's absence is love. Ostensibly the film's ending portrays the situations of Jenny and Dodo as no different if Tad *had* gone abroad, but their happiness and honesty separates the two scenarios.

There are fight scenes within the film but they don't interfere with the flow. This is not the happy-go-lucky Jackie that we have come to know - it is the wild eyed stare of a man turned psychotic with rage. He spares no-one in his personal quest for justice, he never smiles, he rarely follows impressive blows with that little 'Jackie flourish' that normally brings a grin to the face. In many respects he is similar to Ka-Kui of the *Police Story* films, although those films are laced with occasional humour and comic book theatricals.

This is a high quality, believable drama with superb performances all round. Perhaps because it is a more thoughtful work, the film was not a great success world-wide. Popular at home, it won a Hong Kong Film Award for Best Song. This bold and moving film was a 'serious role' blip on Jackie's 1980s films and it would not be until *Crime Story* that he would put on his 'grim face' again. This is a pity because as a film *Heart Of Dragon* is a wonderful achievement from all involved. It is never trite, saccharine or exploitational.

Film Rating: ✪✪✪✪✪
Chan Rating: ✪✪

Police Story (1985)

Director: Jackie Chan

Cast: Jackie Chan, Brigitte Lin, Maggie Cheung, Bill Tung, Chu Yuen

Plot: Operation Boar Hunt is go. The mission: to catch Chu Tao, a notorious night-club owner involved in large drug deals. Ka-Kui (Jackie) catches him after a harrowing chase but the charges are dropped. The police use Salina, Chu Tao's secretary, as a witness for the prosecution. Ka-Kui is charged with protecting her to coax him out. Many double crosses and tragedies later, Ka-Kui has to face the gang, their boss and even the police system itself, for a murder he did not commit, protecting a woman he's hardly met.

Comment: Jackie has often said that *Police Story* was the peak of his career as far as action film directing was concerned. A sweeping comment perhaps, but one that is justifiable. *Police Story* sets out to impress from the very start. Operation Boar Hunt is underway with the police staking out the criminals in a Hong Kong shanty town. Chu Tao and henchmen catch on though, and make their violent escape. They drive through the shanty town to the road below and speed off. That's through the shanty town, buildings crashing, washing lines everywhere, innocent bystanders jumping from the roofs of their (once) homes and all manner of property destruction. Half a million dollars were spent building the town just for Jackie's stuntmen to trash it. Ka-Kui chases Chu Tao and co, eventually forcing them to hijack a bus. He grasps onto the back of it with an umbrella, is dragged behind it and swings like a doll as the bus screeches around corners. When they finally kick him off, he runs after the bus again. Standing in the middle of the road, commandeered car behind him, he aims his gun. The bus driver slams the breaks. The bus stops. Three bad guys crash through the windows and onto the road while Ka-Kui, inches from being hit, arrests Chu Tao. One problem, the stuntmen were meant to land on the car to break their fall. They didn't. It shows.

The film became affectionately(!) known as Glass Story by the huge team of stuntmen employed on the project and it is all too clear to see why. Jackie had discovered sugar-glass as a safer alternative to real glass, and then proceeded to get it made to twice the regular thickness so that it would smash better. And smash it does, particularly in the remarkable shopping mall climax to the picture. People are kicked, spinning, into display units, run head first through cabinets in slow motion or close-up and grabbed by the legs to be dragged through panes of glass. The finale in an already packed feature sees Ka-Kui chasing a villain from the top of the mall to the bottom in one take. Doesn't sound that exciting huh? Well Chu Tao wisely chooses to use the escalator but Ka-Kui, jumps onto a lightbulb-clad pole that runs right through the shopping centre and slides down. Bulbs bursting, he smashes through a display waaaayyy down at the bottom before getting up and apprehending the bad guy. In one take.

The film also contains moments of Jackie humour. Chief brunt of many jokes is Ka-Kui's long-suffering girlfriend May, played by Maggie Cheung. Cheung later became an established star in mad/funny/grim comic strip superhero films like *Heroic Trio* and *Executioners*, and her international work came to attention with her role in *Irma Vep*. May suffers the indignities of having her man turn up with a negligee-clad woman at a surprise party, she is accidentally wrenched off of her moped, she almost gets run over by cars, and ends up getting thrown down stairs. Not that the well-meaning but thoughtless Ka-Kui is any more fortunate - a simple lunchtime meal of noodles in a deserted police station turns into a nightmare as he tries to counsel various victims and explain misunderstandings to May on numerous phones, sliding around the room on his chair and getting the wires in a right tangle.

Bone crunchingly violent and containing the most sustained, impressive and mad stunts, *Police Story* is a truly remarkable film. A landmark in Hong Kong filming, Jackie's career and the whole of the police genre, masterpiece is not an exaggeration.

Injury: Jackie suffered hand abrasions and burns on the pole slide. When setting up the stunt they plugged the bulbs into the mains instead of using a safer low voltage. He also impacted his back.

Film Rating: ✪✪✪✪✪

Chan Rating: ✪✪✪✪

The *Police Story* series rightfully became immensely popular but therein lies a few problems. Firstly, there is the name of Jackie's character himself, it depends which version and which film you are watching – sometimes he's Ka-Kui or Kevin or even Jackie. Secondly there's the numbering – 1 and 2 are fine but from there all manner of things go amiss. *Supercop: Police Story 3* is officially the third film and *First Strike* the fourth but these have been allocated in various countries to *Project S*, *Crime Story* and *Rumble In The Bronx* among others. It's jolly confusing, so watch out.

Armour Of God (1986)

Director: Jackie Chan

Cast: Jackie Chan, Alan Tam, Rosamund Kwan, Lola Forner

Plot: Jackie, aka Asian Hawk, steals a sword worshipped by a primitive tribe. It is one of five parts of the Armour of God which could bring evil to the world. The nasty monks in their cliffside monastery have two of the pieces and kidnap Laura, Asian's ex-girlfriend, to get the other three. This will force him to steal the pieces, which now reside in the collection of a rich baron, Asian having sold the sword in auction. Asian and Alan, Laura's current boyfriend, eventually borrow the pieces to get her back. But they have to be accompanied by May, the baron's daughter and self-confessed markswoman. Infiltrating the monastery they save Laura, not realising that she's been drugged as part of a fiendish plan. So Asian has to rescue them again and also save the whole of the Armour of God, and the world!

Comment: Often described as an Asian *Indiana Jones*, *Armour Of God* sees Chan experimenting with a more international feel to his pictures. This film was huge, and consolidated his position as the number one action-comedy star, breaking all existing Hong Kong records. Like both *James Bond* and *Indiana Jones*, the film has a gratuitous pre-credit sequence. Jackie steals the Sword of God by abseiling to its honoured place. This grace is countered by clumsiness as the head of a statue falls over and he is spotted. After temporarily fooling the natives into thinking he's a deity, they chase after him, throwing spears as he jumps across burning coals before swinging through a ruin and sliding down a mountainside on a borrowed shield, whilst being followed by an irate horde. Our hero finally escapes in a kit form plane cunningly disguised as a bush. This is one of the many Bond-style gadgets that he uses in the film. Others include an exploding can of Kirin beer and a Mitsubishi with a mini escape pod!

The film's climax begins with Hawk abseiling down a ridiculously large cliff on the mountainside in order to reach the monks' secret cave. Then follows a riotous confrontation featuring four stiletto-clad she-vixens in a truly astonishing piece of choreography. The sheer delight of the scene resides in the decision to use, à la *Fantasy Mission Force*, beefy male stand-ins. It's a scream. In one shot Jackie is kicked by a leg that is about twice as thick as his whole body! After that we have him decked in dynamite (a bit like Godard's *Pierrot Le Fou*) igniting the sticks threateningly, then trying desperately to put them out (ironic as in the out-takes he has trouble getting them lit) and in the meantime wrecking the whole place and stealing the armour. If you're not happy with that, how about having him jump from the aforementioned cave onto a passing hot air balloon to be drifted away to safety?

Some may find the longer comedy moments a little slow. These include the scene where the four heroes are all in the same hotel, in and out of rooms and in and out of love with each other, all the time unaware that May is under the influence of a mind drug. Overall though, *Armour Of God* is a strange hybrid of genres, and works so well because it blends them all up into one delicious coulis of a film.

Injury: The opening, incredible as it is, nearly cost him his life. Jumping from one wall to another, using a branch as a swing, the branch broke and Jackie fell. The cameraman below ran and Jackie smashed his head on a rock. Rushed to the nearest hospital (they were filming in Yugoslavia) Jackie was saved but there is still a hole in his skull that remains vulnerable to this day. The whole thing is shown, silent, at the end of the film with the other 'bloopers' and is sobering.

Film Rating: ✪✪✪✪
Chan Rating: ✪✪✪✪✪

Project A Part 2 (1987)

Director: Jackie Chan

Cast: Jackie Chan, Maggie Cheung, David Lam, Rosamund Kwan, Bill Tung

Plot: Dragon Ma is back. This time he takes over the police force's West District from Superintendent Chan, who seems to be rather too involved with some of the local ruffians. Ma's out to reform the police force and win over his new colleagues by capturing some wicked criminals. He also becomes involved with a bunch of Chinese revolutionaries who set him up as a thief, but eventually see the error of their ways. Added to all this, he is being pursued by some disgruntled pirates who are not entirely happy that he was responsible for the demise of their leader.

Comment: Although the *Project A* films do not necessarily contain the most action or the longest set-pieces, they are without doubt among Jackie's most consistent films. Continuing straight on from the original, Dragon Ma and his chums and the one honest policeman in the district, battle together to get rid of the corrupt cops and nasty criminals. Ma is the archetypal Chan hero – a good guy, honest and brave enough to stand up for his beliefs, and a mighty fine fighter should the going get rough. Superintendent Chan on the other hand is outwardly respectable and inwardly devious, and conveniently catches criminals just as the newspaper reporters turn up. He is also ruthless and quite content to dispatch anyone in his path.

The set-pieces include the action-packed arrest of gang boss Tiger, and a hilarious pursuit involving Ma, handcuffed to Superintendent Chan, trying to escape the axe-wielding pirates who are both angry and hungry. But the comic highlight of the proceedings is the scene where Maggie Cheung has to simultaneously entertain five sets of guests, from all the different political groups (some of whom are handcuffed to each other), at her house, whilst desperately ensuring that none of them meet each other. This is pure Marx Brothers. Indeed, everything harks back to the early days of cinema, and not just in the beautifully reproduced setting of turn-of-the-century Hong Kong. The visual comedy is superb - the scene in which Ma is sneaking around the Ambassador's house looking for jewel thieves is great - when the light falls upon him, he freezes imitating a character in the Rembrandt painting behind him, which is appropriate the first time and very silly the second. The gags too are of the old school, but benefit from Jackie's adaptations. They include the classic 'remove the

55

tablecloth while the crockery remains intact, whilst dispatching a disgruntled pirate' routine and a 'whipping a chair away from the pirate so he falls over' feat. Being Jackie, it is all performed incredibly quickly and with perfect comic timing. Debt is also owed directly to Buster Keaton's *Steamboat Bill Jr* (as it was to Harold Lloyd in the original *Project A*) in the final scene, where Jackie literally brings the house down as he runs down the side of an enormous falling ceremonial wall and another collapses right on top of him, his head passing through a paper window.

The climax is awesome - our hero is initially thrown into an industrial mortar and has to dodge the giant pestle while his enemies pour oil over the side. Escaping by cunningly catching an adversary's tie, he then has to hide the revolutionaries' incriminating book. Fighting his opponents over bamboo scaffolding, he jumps over rooftops, and almost drowns in a fish hatchery before the final confrontation.

The *Project A* films are without doubt amongst Jackie's best. They seamlessly blend action and comedy and the period setting ensures that they haven't dated one bit. He even sings the theme tune at the end as the credits roll.

Injuries: When Jackie eats chilli, then spits the juice onto his hands and wipes them in the eyes of his enemies he had to use real chillies. Hot stuff!

Film Rating: ✪✪✪✪✪
Chan Rating: ✪✪✪✪✪

Dragons Forever (1988)

Director: Samo Hung

Cast: Jackie Chan, Samo Hung, Yuen Biao, Dick Wei, Benny 'The Jet' Urquidez

Plot: Johnny Lung (Jackie) is a womaniser and lacks morals which makes him ideal lawyer material. He is hired to defend Mr Wah against Miss Yeh, whose fish lake is being polluted with Wah's chemical dying factory. Hiring Luke (Samo) and the neurotic Tim (Yuen Biao) to gather information on Miss Yeh and her expert Miss Lee, proves to be a bad idea leading to fights, romance, break-ups and betrayals all around. Johnny tries to convince everyone that he is righteous, and it becomes abundantly clear that the factory is not what it seems. It's not the clothes that are dying...

Comment: At the time of writing this is the last film that the 'heroic trio' performed together, rather ironic considering the title. Director

Samo's choice of character for Jackie is an unusual one, by casting him as a lawyer who thinks only of money and women. Ultimately the film hinges on Johnny's redemption but, until the ending, he is more a linch-pin upon which the rest of the madness hangs. As well as having to defend himself physically in a couple of fights, he also has to prove his worth as a lawyer. In a moment of legal insanity he asks Miss Lee, in court, under oath, whether she loves him as this will affect the case. To add emphasis to the decision the judge utters the immortal line "You may be an oceanographic expert but you are also a woman."

Samo plays Luke, initially introduced to us as an arms-dealer and despite his prodigious fighting talents, restricts his combative role to brief skirmishes with his buddies. He does get to woo Miss Yeh, winning her over with irritating perseverance and a big megaphone. Yuen Biao is in his element as the neurotic friend and is given ample opportunity to create an entirely deranged persona. Tim's visits to his psychiatrist play a vital part in his character's descent into madness. Eventually, he can only speak to his shrink by intercom – except its really a robber who has tied up the staff and advises Tim to destroy the witnesses to a crime he worries about, including Jackie and co.

In other films, the trio rarely fought each other, but in *Dragons Forever* they lay into each other hammer and tongs. In one classic sequence, Miss Lee and Johnny are trying to enjoy a romantic dinner at his apartment, but Luke is already there, forcing Johnny to hide him. When a totally nuts Tim arrives, it is all Johnny can do to keep them from killing each other, and revealing their presence. Eventually he can cope no longer and speeds up Miss Lee's departure; however she needs to return to collect her coat, each time finding Johnny further bruised by his rapidly failing attempts at peacemaker. Later, when their deception towards Misses Lee and Yeh is discovered, the three have a huge punch-up in a car park where the fists and feet start flying. If you thought the prospect of the three brothers fighting against each other makes for exciting viewing then wait 'til you see them fight together at film's climax. Samo takes out about a dozen guys in spectacular fashion but is finally defeated by the appearance of our old pal Benny 'The Jet' Urquidez, whose awesome fighting prowess is matched here by his amusingly overdone eye make-up. It is then down to the Chan and Yuen duo to save the day. The factory is suitably hazardous and, unsurprisingly, a lot of the action takes place above ground floor, facilitating some of the most painful looking falls and near-misses yet. Many henchmen are thrown from windows to solid ground in a single take or slammed headfirst into concrete. When the big fight is on, Jackie gets another shot at Benny. It's a great bout and in many ways more satisfying than *Wheels On Meals*.

Dragons Forever is a stonking ride of a film. If there is a problem, it lies with the treatment of the central female characters who basically serve as victims, even in the comedy sequences. The magnificent ending and general pacing are superb and as a vehicle for the trio to bow out together, it is great fun and recommended viewing.

Injury: Impacted ankle from fighting Benny

Film Rating: ✪✪✪✪

Chan Rating: ✪✪✪

Police Story II (1988)

Director: Jackie Chan

Cast: Jackie Chan, Maggie Cheung, Bill Tung, Lam Kwok-Hung

Plot: Chu Tao has been released from prison on compassionate grounds - threatening Ka-Kui (Jackie) with the help of his smarmy lawyer and greasy henchmen. Ka-Kui's bosses Inspector Chang (aka Uncle Bill) and Raymond are unimpressed by his heroics and put him back on the beat. Meanwhile May, his long-suffering girlfriend, is being intimidated and some terrorists bomb a shopping arcade, demanding a ransom to stop their campaign. With his love-life in tatters, the ransom increasing, May kidnapped and a waistcoat full of explosives strapped to his chest, Ka-Kui's prospects are not looking good…

Comment: Hong Kong's capacity to soak up sequels is unsurpassed so it was only a matter of time before Jackie would return to this popular series. *Police Story II* however, is a far darker and more complex affair than its predecessor. Early in the proceedings Ka-Kui is hit with a double-whammy – his bosses are unhappy because of his antics, and his nemesis Chu Tao has been released from prison because he apparently has only three months to live. Mocking our hero from the safety of his chauffeur driven car, apparently ailment-free, the audience's conclusion is the same as Ka-Kui's – Chu Tao got out of gaol free. Later, when Ka-Kui confronts the ageing boss hooked up to a hospital machine, genuinely sick, our expectations are confounded. When Ka-Kui attacks his dying nemesis, our loyalties still lie with him but are sorely tested by our social outrage at a strong young man torturing a sick OAP. What is interesting is that in *Police Story* we unquestioningly accepted Ka-Kui's flagrant disregard for law and police procedure because he fulfils the man-on-the-edge criteria so beloved of the genre. In *Police Story II* we are forced to confront the possibility that not only is Ka-Kui wrong but he is a sociopath with an ego gone mad.

The complexity of the film also lies within its skilful manipulation of audience expectations and desires. When Ka-Kui, currently out of the force, takes it on board to evacuate the shopping arcade following a bomb threat we are torn. On the one hand, we don't want the bomb to explode because of the loss of life and order that it represents. On the other hand, we want the bomb to explode, because if it doesn't Ka-Kui is going to be spending a lot of time behind bars for evacuating a shopping centre without authority. The scenes outside the arcade are excruciating - you are willing the place to blow, just as a little boy's ball bounces into the now-deserted forecourt. In a marvellous moment of tension, music and elongated editing, Ka-Kui fetches the ball which bounces ominously in slow motion. The audience now doesn't want the place blow, until he's out of harm's way. It is a truly wonderful scene, perfectly punctuated with suspense and fluctuating emotions. Similarly, when Ka-Kui is tortured by May's kidnappers, these petty tormentors read out May's rejection letter to him. It's a terrible moment, showing two people in love, pulled apart by his duty and dedication, at the mercy of people without souls. They are both in tears and this dissection of the human condition and frailty is what gives it such power.

Naturally, being a Jackie Chan film there are fight scenes galore – *Police Story II*, while not attaining the level of sustained violence of its predecessor, is no slouch, opting instead for some highly inventive, compact sequences that are among Chan's very best. The highlight fight occurs when May and Jackie are attacked in a children's adventure playground. It is one of Jackie's all-time great fight sequences as every piece of the park is used. The irony that playgrounds are meant to be safe fun places for kids seems to have been lost as the crunch rate increases. Following a horrendous torture sequence with thundercrackers, our scarred hero is forced to be a human bomb to get the ransom, then return to Fong's Warehouse to dispatch the rotters who have May. This involves some outrageous bus stunts, several bouts of fisticuffs, a nasty encounter with a forklift truck and far too many barrels. May finally escapes down a flimsy plastic tube but Ka-Kui's descent is accompanied by a bomb which explodes half way. You really won't believe your eyes!

While comedy is not at the forefront of this particular film, it is present, although the effect counterpoints the pathos as often as it produces laughs. When May is deported from Bali following Ka-Kui's reinstatement, she confronts him in the men's locker room, oblivious to the naked men around her and to Uncle Bill sitting on the toilet.

Not to everyone's taste, *Police Story II* is the darkest of the series. There is relatively little comedy and a fair bit of introspection, self-doubt and dilemma. Morally complex yet sacrificing none of the excitement of his lighter works, this is one of his best films. Credit for this remarkable film is also due to Edward Tang who, with Jackie, has written some of his best stories.

Injury: Jackie, crossing a main road to confront the baddies is hit by a van prior to the encounter. He took the take a few times as the van was not getting quite close enough to achieve the correct level of realism. On the final take the driver went slightly too close and Jackie ended up in hospital – "good shot" he recalls. If jumping from a lorry to a bus and dodging signs is not enough, Jackie dives through a glass sign. Unfortunately he dived through the wrong pane and ended up with a head full of glass. This is on top of a very nasty head gash following a bungled chair-throwing stunt, shards of firecracker in the eye and a badly-damaged back following a bar fall. On *Police Story II*, however, it was also his female co-star who was injured. Maggie Cheung had her head split severely following her stunt - running through toppling metal frames at the film's climax.

Film Rating: ✪✪✪✪✪
Chan Rating: ✪✪✪✪✪

Miracles (aka Mr Canton And Lady Rose, The Canton Godfather) (1989)

Director: Jackie Chan

Cast: Jackie Chan, Anita Mui, Billy Tung, Richard Ng, Jackie Cheung

Plot: Kuo Chen Wah (Jackie) is out of work but spends his last cents on a lucky rose. He accidentally becomes a gang godfather and part owner of the Ritz hotel. Rival gangs want the other half of the business, originally owned by the father of Lu Ming Yang (Mui). Miss Yang becomes the Ritz's singer as they transform the establishment into a

60

night-club. All the time Kuo is trying to run a 'nice' Mafia operation, something his own gang can't get their heads around, let alone other gangs and the police. Attempting to be really virtuous, Kuo arranges for the Rose Lady Madame Kao to continue a charade that enables her to look rich, so that her daughter can be happily married. But perhaps he relies as much on her as she does on him.

Comment: *Miracles* is Jackie's self-confessed favourite film, an unrepentantly sentimental and nostalgic look at 1930s Hong Kong unencumbered by any political subtext. In terms of the sumptuous art direction, the composition and structure it is hard to disagree with his assertion. This is a wonderful feel-good film in the mould of Frank Capra (it is based in part on *Lady For A Day* (1933) and *A Pocket Full Of Miracles* (1954) and reflects Capra's grasp of innocence in a cynical world) but also contains elements of Coppola's *The Godfather* (1970) and Busby Berkley musicals!

Golden Harvest relented on a genuinely personal project for Jackie - one for which they would foot an incredible budget. The only stipulation was that there had to be some scenes of action. *Miracles* was huge. Half a mountainside was demolished to construct the massive recreation of old Hong Kong and one shot alone took three days to set up. Nine months were spent shooting the film to Jackie's increasingly exacting standards. The cinematography sparkles - in one astonishing single take, as the club is being decorated, the camera glides over and around all the proceedings, catching Jackie narrowly missing being hit by a falling fan and continues to survey the surroundings. There are many of these throughout the film, recreating the grandeur of classical Hollywood cinema.

There is truly something for everyone in *Miracles* - pathos, rags-to-riches, situation comedy and intrigue. And yes, stunt and fight fans, Jackie has not forgotten you either. *Miracles*, surprisingly, also features some of his most inventive scenes of mayhem yet. When we first come across the gangsters they are arguing over ownership of the Ritz, bullets are swapped and a car chase ensues, sedans flying everywhere. One painful-looking stunt has the poor unfortunate falling down some spiral stairs, all the time bumping his unmentionables. Ouch. The real highlight though is a superb rickshaw sequence that will leave you gasping. Following a punch-up at a barbers, Jackie gets onto a rickshaw tied to the back of a car and hurtles through the streets. However, the bad guys are around, so more fisticuffs result and a market load of prickly fruit turn into some surprising projectiles.

At heart *Miracles* is a comedy of manners (the gangsters learning etiquette is priceless) about a man who wants to do good against the odds. It is not the all-out manic fight-a-thon that Jackie's followers have come to expect, but rather a Sunday afternoon film for all the family. Additional pleasure can be derived from the subtitled song which includes such immortal lines as "The quintessence of Regal excitement" and the unforgettable "My love tentacles reach out to hold you." Marvellous.

Injury: Cut his eye on the bamboo handle of the rickshaw. Gashed his hand on an axe handle.

Film Rating: ✪✪✪✪✪

Chan Rating: ✪✪✪✪

Operation Condor: Armour Of God II (1990)

Director: Jackie Chan

Cast: Jackie Chan, Carol Cheng, Eva Cobo de Garcia, Shoko Ikeda, Ken Lo, Vincent Lyn

Plot: Our hero Jackie, aka Asian Condor, is called in by the UN, via the Duke, to help recover some Nazi gold hidden in the Sahara. Accompanying him will be Ada (the Duke's prim aide), the granddaughter of one of the Nazis, and a Japanese hippie with a pet scorpion called Ding Ding. The task is not simple. Heading from Morocco to the Sahara, our intrepid band have to contend with two inept Arab assassins, a group of mercenaries and the wheelchair bound Eighteenth Nazi, Adolph. The hidden gold awaits honest distribution through the UN or the greedy pockets of selfish men...

Comment: *Miracles* had cost Golden Harvest a tidy packet, but audiences were still not ready for a romantic period piece - Jackie Chan meant Jackie action. As a result of this, a decision was made to resurrect the popular Asian Hawk character (and inexplicably rename him Asian Condor) for a further set of adventures. If Golden Harvest had thought that *Miracles* was pricey, they were in for a shock. For not the first (or last) time in his career, Jackie would create the most expensive Hong Kong film made. Logistically the film was huge. Three months were spent shooting in the Sahara, braving bad weather, disease and 'uncooperative food,' as well as the normal life-threatening stunts. In the end they had to recreate part of it in Hong Kong with imported sand because the conditions were so harsh. The Morocco section ended up a disaster with the production manager being put in prison for distributing counterfeit money - the fake money used in the film.

To improve the international appeal of the film, three female leads were used, from China, Japan and Europe. Jackie's own appeal is, naturally, universal. Notable set-pieces include the fight involving bumbling Arab twins as they unwittingly save Jackie and companions from the really bad guys, with bodies flying from balconies, and an out-of-control machine gun. Far more satisfying is the noble sacrifice performed by Ding Ding the scorpion as Jackie fakes poisoning to avoid death, while Ada and the granddaughter are taken into slavery. Their subsequent rescue is a hysterical sequence involving a Mitsubishi (naturally) pulling down a tent while a subtly disguised Jackie tries to buy the girls, earning himself a painful kick in the privates for his troubles.

The climax of the film sees an underground fight for the Nazi gold, along metal ledges and across painful-looking pipes. At its most frenetic it resembles *Dragons Forever* though not quite as intense. What *Dragons Forever* didn't have was a huge wind tunnel in which the stars could be thrown hither and thither – Jackie taking on Ken Lo and Vincent Lyn in a face warping, high flying, death defying bout of sheer lunacy. Some of the grotesque faces pulled in these extreme conditions are well worth a freeze frame.

Ultimately if there is a problem with the *Armour Of God* films it is because they try too hard to appeal to an international audience at the expense of giving people what they want - Jackie. *Operation Condor* goes further down the epic track that was started with *Armour Of God* and reached its pinnacle with *First Strike*, where the slapstick and violence are replaced by situation and scale.

Injury: The falling chain dropping Jackie a sizeable distance onto what looks like concrete in the closing credits must have hurt. He also received a puncture wound to the leg.

Film Rating: ✪✪✪✪
Chan Rating: ✪✪✪✪

Island On Fire (1991)

Director: Chu Yen-Ping

Cast: Jackie Chan, Tony Leung, Andy Lau, Samo Hung, Jimmy Wang Yu

Plot: Policeman Andy is persuaded to do an undercover job in a prison. In the slammer he shares his cell with mouse owner Charlie. The cook, played by Samo, repeatedly launches escape plans in order to see his young son. Steve (Jackie) finds himself inside after accidentally killing the brother of Lee, who now wants revenge. All find some protection from Lucas, the prison Mafia head. Life is harsh inside, resulting in many deaths. But are the deceased really dead and is there an even more fiendish plan to reveal?

Comment: Jimmy Wang Yu called upon Jackie for a second time as a special favour to help put some extra star presence into his latest venture, a grim prison film with a title echoing Ringo Lam's popular *On Fire* series.

Life in the prison is harsh and the fighting every Saturday is brutal and bloody. It is clear who to side with from the outset, with perhaps the exception of Lucas (Jimmy Wang Yu) a tattooed Triad whose benevolence seems at odds with the rest of his character. Jackie himself is a contradiction in this one. *Island On Fire* is a landmark film - the only one where Jackie dies several times! Our first encounter sees Jackie as a pool player unwilling to take a fall, a mistake that leaves his girlfriend critically injured and means he faces life for murder. A later fight with Lee's brother, who bought his way into prison for personal revenge, happens under the watchful eyes of the prisoners and warders. Jackie and Lee go at it like mad, climbing up stairways and clashing knives. The final scenes are another rarity for Chan. After some fisticuffs, our resurrected heroes gun down half the military in their attempt to escape, having been hired as an assassination squad for a vigilante group of highly dubious moral persuasion. Seeing Jackie with a gun in favour of fists is rare enough, but to have him blasting pounds of flesh from a seemingly endless stream of militia is disconcerting to say the least.

Island On Fire is not a typical Chan film - there is no humour in it for one thing. Irritatingly, the overall premise is fascinating, but the resolution is glossed over all too quickly – as if they wanted to dwell more upon the seedy prison life than a fascinating conspiracy plot.

However it is entertaining, occasionally mad, and exciting. You won't regret watching this, just don't expect large crazy stunts and madcap tomfoolery.

Film Rating: ✪✪✪
Chan Rating: ✪✪

Twin Dragons (1991)

Director: Tsui Hark & Ringo Lam

Cast: Jackie Chan, Maggie Cheung, almost every director in Hong Kong

Plot: Following a hospital siege, twin babies are separated. Years later, one has grown up as a world famous conductor and pianist, the other a seedy car mechanic. Fate being what it is, their paths cross. Jackie Chan films being what they are, comedy and action are not far behind as the pair are repeatedly mistaken for each other.

Comment: Jackie's contributions to charities are renowned – his Jackie Chan Foundation performs great work, mainly for children. Additionally, Jackie's work as a director and stuntman has led him to be honoured with several prominent roles in the film industry. Chief among these is head of the Directors Guild of Hong Kong, who at the time required headquarters for their operations. This is where *Twin Dragons* comes in. Rather than arranging a jumble sale, they made a film to raise money. In the spirit of the film, twin directors were employed - Tsui Hark who was instrumental in the modernisation of the Hong Kong film industry, introducing awesome special effects with the incredible *Zu: Warriors From The Magic Mountain* (1982), reinventing the martial arts film with *Once Upon A Time In China* (1991) and the swordplay film in *Swordsman* (1990), and his *Peking Opera Blues* (1986) remains a pinnacle of cinema. Joining Hark was Ringo Lam, maker of the *On Fire* films, the first of which (*City On Fire* (1987)) provided the inspiration for *Reservoir Dogs* (1992), the insane *Full Contact* (1992) and the hugely underrated gore-drenched *Burning Paradise* (1994).

Retelling Shakespeare's *Comedy Of Errors* with two Jackie Chans sounds like a lot of fun and it is, even though Jackie was extensively body doubled in this film. Much of the comedy is derived from mistaken identity, and additional mileage is gained by having an empathetic link between the twins. This is wonderfully foreshadowed in the early concert scenes of a madly gesticulating Jackie as a dynamic conductor, under the influence of his twin who is currently involved in a fight. This resonates later on when the pair use their linking to great advantage, as our mild-mannered conductor gets to slug it out like a bruiser pro.

Tsui Hark is used to effects filmmaking, but *Twin Dragons* is sadly not one of his better efforts. Generally he tends to concentrate on fast edits and whip cuts to accentuate the movement of the action, but *Twin Dragons* relies more often on the two Jackies being on screen at the same time, a far more subtle and long winded technique. Jackie has often spoken of his in-and-out of costumes excursions on this film, and doesn't remember them too fondly!

Undoubtedly fun to watch and with lots to see, *Twin Dragons* is a great piece of family entertainment, but as a film it's a bit of a mess. Hark, Lam and Chan have all made better films in their own individual styles, so perhaps it's this hodgepodge of ideas that lets the film down. It would be mean to be overly critical and regardless, the film made a profit and even gained a limited, if overdue, cinema release in the UK. Meanwhile, in Kowloon, the prestigious new offices of the Directors Guild remain conspicuous by their absence.

Film Rating: ✪✪
Chan Rating: ✪✪✪

Police Story III: Supercop (1992)

Director: Stanley Tong

Cast: Jackie Chan, Michelle Yeoh, Maggie Cheung, Bill Tung

Plot: Ka-Kui (Jackie of course) is sent on a special mission to China, working with their Supercop (Michelle Yeoh) to break up a sinister drugs cartel. Even May can't know of the mission. The trail leads, via some devious undercover subterfuge, back to Hong Kong and eventually to Malaysia. There they accidentally bump into the suitably disgruntled May and the scene is set for a stunning climax against the evil druglords...

Comment: Golden Harvest were still keeping their biggest asset in front of the camera rather than behind it to cope with the demand for his films, so they hired the up-and-coming director Stanley Tong. Tong had worked his way swiftly up the ranks of stunt performer and choreographer eventually to become Jackie's favourite director because of his attention to stunt detail. Tong, you see, performs all of the stunts in his films prior to any stunt man involvement, to test that the routine is safe. In his work, the comedy element is more visual and less classical and there is also much emphasis on vehicular stunts, a throwback to his days on *Angel 2* (1989). Apart from his work with Jackie, his talents can be seen in the television series *Martial Law* with Samo Hung, which he produces and occasionally directs. *Police Story 3* sees the return of Michelle Yeoh (previously Khan) after a five year absence from the screen. She is probably best known for her role in *Tomorrow Never Dies* (1997), outclassing Pierce Brosnan's James Bond, but had been making films in Hong Kong for years. She can even be seen briefly in *Twinkle, Twinkle Lucky Stars* but became famous for her hard hitting (literally!) roles in *Yes Madam* (1985) and *Royal Warriors* (1986). She is perhaps the only person to come close to upstaging Jackie in one of his own films. The action set-pieces are mad even by Jackie's standards, but show a change of direction into more hardware orientated stunts. Thus, despite a commendable number of fist slinging scenes, this doesn't approach the intense brutality of the first *Police Story* films. For the last time Maggie Cheung returns as May, but her role is limited and newcomers to the series could well be confused as to her status in Ka-Kui's life.

Working undercover, Ka-Kui is admitted to a Chinese coal mining prison where he assists the escape of Panther. Tong's use of scale in the context of the stunning scenery as the pair run after a carriage on a mountain and then death slide down the other side, is exemplary. Ka-Kui is then invited to join Panther and the rest of the criminals and they travel to meet his 'family,' his new partner playing his 'sister' and Uncle Bill his 'mother,' complete with the essential comedy breasts that always accompany such cross-dressing! Supercop Michelle saves our hero in a restaurant fight in stunning style - double and triple kicking and spinning like a Dervish, so she too joins the gang. The criminals go to their secret location for the drugs deal. It will come as no surprise to learn that the police follow them, and chaos ensues as the whole camp is decimated by bazooka fire and dynamite. This sequence highlights the major differences in Tong's use of camera and style of action making. It is more operatic and chaotic, overblown and grandiose to the balletic personal touch that Chan normally uses. There are explosions, gun fire, some buddy-buddy shooting routines with Michelle and Jackie that really work.

The finale is breathtaking in its scale and escalation. Cheng Wen-Shi, the drug lord's wife, has been sentenced to death but is freed in a devious rescue. The chase is on. She escapes by helicopter, but Jackie clutches on to the dangling rope ladder and is taken on a whirlwind tour of Kuala Lumpa. Seeing Jackie hang on for all he's worth, being rammed into advertising boards and managing to sail inches above buildings, before being dragged through the steam of an oncoming train is a sight to behold. There are no CGI helicopters here. For the shooting, the pilot could not see his swinging cargo and had to rely on verbal instructions to ensure Jackie's safety. Why would someone be willing to do such a relentlessly dangerous and virtually uncontrollable stunt? The answer is because Michelle Yeoh had been so dynamic, brave and, let's face it, stupid that Jackie had to go one better. Michelle had pulled off an incredible motorcycle jump onto a moving train despite having learnt how to ride the bike only two days previously, so Jackie felt compelled to top that! The train-top fight is another winner with Jackie at one point swinging around an overhanging water pipe to avoid his foe - but there's also a helicopter blade to dodge. In the first take Jackie didn't quite miss the helicopter and ended up injured again.

Supercop lacks the emotional pull that made the first films masterpieces, but it gains two of the most talented stunt stars to grace the screen. It gives an indication of this trend towards more 'wholesome' family orientated fare while retaining the dramatic pacing. Awesome fun, but more shallow than its brothers.

Injury: Getting hit by a helicopter resulting in a badly bruised back, dislocated cheekbone.

Film Rating: ✪✪✪✪
Chan Rating: ✪✪✪

City Hunter (1993)

Director: Wong Jing

Cast: Jackie Chan, Chingmy Yau, Richard Norton

Plot: Ryu (Jackie) aka City Hunter, a private detective, daydreamer and womaniser is set the task of rescuing a millionaire's daughter who has run away from home. He finds her at a skateboarding park but soon loses her again. The clues point to an expensive cruise liner. On board, a group of terrorists plan to rob the passengers of their valuables, oh, and kill them all too. His partner Kari (his dead buddy's daughter), her bumbling would-be boyfriend, a bevy of beautiful women and a killer card thrower all team up to overthrow the evil criminals.

Comment: Wong Jing is one of Hong Kong's most prolific writer/directors with a string of popular hits under his belt. *City Hunter* is based on the successful Japanese manga of the same name and was seen as a way of appeasing the multitude of Japanese fans. Ryu of the Manga is not only ruthless, he's also a promiscuous cad, so the character needed lightening up. Jing's approach was to make the film a comic book come to life – ridiculously bright colours, outrageous angles and juvenile visual gags. One aspect of the comic that does remain (although not frequently enough) is a diminutive City Hunter being bashed over the head with an unfeasibly large mallet by a disgruntled Kari.

City Hunter may lack the careful, planned, realistic feel of Chan's 1980s work (there are a lot of wire shots on show and a great deal of special effects work - not something Chan is fond of) but this is replaced by a manic chaos of day-glo stupidity that is easy to enjoy. There are so many set-pieces it's hard to know where to start. The skateboard chase with Jackie boarding over cars chased by youths against the flow of the traffic has to be seen to be believed. Then there's the cinema brawl, Jackie taking hints from Bruce Lee in *Game Of Death* (1978) in how to defeat an opponent twice his size. Not content with fist fights there are gun fights with red-suited storm troopers, some impressive card throwing from a *God Of Gamblers* (1990) style good guy, some lecherous stupidity involving breasts appearing as hamburgers (don't ask) and the most ridiculous duel in screen history. Arch bad guy (Richard Norton in a wince-inducing muscles 'n' splits role) is against our man Ryu in the amusement arcade section of the ship. As a *Street Fighter II* console gets trashed, he turns into Ken and Jackie, electrocuted, has to defeat him by adopting the guise of other characters from the game. The final victory blow is reserved for China's Chun Li – Jackie doing a sterling impression complete with ponytails, bobby socks and fetching dress.

At the end of the day, *City Hunter* is an acquired taste that will certainly alienate some of Jackie's fanbase, but if taken in the right spirit is a totally barmy exhilarating romp. Take off your serious hat and enjoy yourself.

Injury: Dislocated shoulder, damaged knees during the skateboard chase

Film Rating: ✪✪✪✪
Chan Rating: ✪✪✪

Crime Story (1993)

Director: Kirk Wong

Cast: Jackie Chan, Kent Cheng, Poon Ling-Ling, Blackie Ko, Ken Lo

Plot: Mr Wong, property developer and generally bad guy, is kidnapped and held to ransom, his wife released to get the money. On the case are Eddie Chan (Jackie) and Hong, but unbeknownst to our law abiding cop, Hong is corrupt and one of the perpetrators of the kidnap. The pair travel to Taiwan for the laundered money and to capture implicated terrorist Simon Ting but are not only up against the criminals, but the police too. Will Chan save Mr Wong and expose Hong?

Comment: Director Kirk Wong had a reputation for producing tough and grim pictures, usually with a blurring of morality and a story from the headlines. He had spent a couple of years developing *Crime Story* when his contracted star, Jet Li, had to leave the production. Jackie stepped in, relishing the chance to play a straight role again. Structurally similar to the director's *Rock 'n' Roll Cop* (1994), with Taiwan replacing China, *Crime Story* is based on a true story, emphasised in the closing testament to police officers who had died investigating kidnappings.

Jackie's character is a good cop, but an unhappy one. When forced to protect Wong, the capitalist property developer, he does so and disperses Wong's irate workers with diplomacy and not force. Chan is also willing to put his life and reputation on the line to protect Wong and his wife. He risks all for his fellow officers - when one is killed on a motorbike in a horrific and deliberate crash, Chan risks his own life to prevent the same thing happening to another. This is where *Crime Story* really shows its metal. Chan's attempt to save the injured motorcycle cop extends to a melodramatic ride to the hospital and painful agonising with the relations. Likewise, the kidnapping itself is brutal and swift - in order to get the money the kidnappers need Mrs Wong alive, but her weak heart gives out on her. The solution? Jump-start her with a car battery.

Despite the low-key and depressing edge to the film, there are some great action sequences to enjoy – the car chases have a *Mad Max* (1979) immediacy and one particular motorbike crash looks horrific. The confrontations between Chan and Hong are frightening and the climactic fight features some truly nasty moments. But the real coup de grace comes with the destruction of the buildings - Chan running through the exploding brickwork as though his life depended upon it. It did. This protracted series of destruction is incredibly realistic - filmed at the location where the buildings really were due to be demolished. A stroke of luck that goes a long way to explaining the realism of the piece.

Crime Story is a good movie - it is interesting to see Chan in a non-comedy role and he proves himself more than capable in the many scenes of pathos and introspection. It may be that, as he gets older, these grittier parts will become the norm for him as the physical demands are not as relentless as the average Chan comedy. Alternatively we may see a lighter, more romantic Chan emerge as in *Gorgeous*.

Injury: Legs crushed between two cars.

Film Rating: ✪✪✪✪

Chan Rating: ✪✪

Drunken Master II (1995)

Director: Lau Kar Lueng & Jackie Chan

Cast: Jackie Chan, Anita Mui, Ti Lung, Ken Lo

Plot: Wong Fei Hung (Jackie) faces trouble on a train when his father's ginseng gets swapped with a rare piece of jade. His father, Wong Kei-Ying, is approached to sell his land for use by the local mining company whose boss exploits the workers ruthlessly. Fei Hung is well-meaning, but his reliance on alcohol to fuel his fighting skills is frowned upon. Devious plans are hatched to force Wong Kei-Ying give up his land and eventually it is up to Fei Hung to deal with matters, even if it means breaking his vow…

Comment: Fifteen years since his original star turn, Jackie reprises the character and also makes his first traditional kung fu film for over a decade. There was a surprising resurgence in the genre in the wake of Tsui Hark's patriotic and engrossing *Once Upon A Time In China* films. What set Hark's film apart was the masterful use of cinematography and editing to portray the people's hero as almost superhuman. Many of the stunning fight sequences had relied heavily on wirework to accentuate movement, but Jackie always relied upon the abilities of the performers rather than the skill of the technicians and could legitimately reinvent Wong Fei Hung from this perspective. What *Drunken Master II* managed to do was to bring the new wave martial arts sensibilities into a film without compromising the integrity of the traditional movie. Early on, Fei Hung faces a spear-wielding guard, underneath a train. The speed and dexterity of the staged spear dodging is a staple of both the martial arts film and Peking opera. This is enhanced by the constricted 'stage' of the railtracks in a breathtaking display - there is no visible trickery so you can marvel at the performer's skills without suspicion.

Later in his life, Wong Fei Hung became a sombre and righteous individual with a strong knowledge of Chinese medicine, traits he learned from his well-meaning and traditional father. But it is undoubtedly his mother who added the zest and impetuosity to his persona. A fierce mah jong player (much to her husbands chagrin) she lifts the film, providing it with lashings of humour. She is also a proficient martial artist, getting a good opportunity to show off her skills. When we first see Fei Hung let out the full might of his drunken style, it is to avenge his mother. Laying into his foe, he re-emphasises his pledge "Dad won't let me drink" - but mum chucks him some booze with the reply "I will!" The swift inebriation of our protagonist becomes increasingly outrageous as, in addition to his spectacular wielding of bench, foot and fist, he also has to catch additional 'inspiration' pitched by his expert mum. You'd be hard-pressed to find a funnier or more exciting scene, as our hero does goalkeeper-style brandy bottle saves, pokes people in the eyes, gets as drunk as a skunk and even attacks his own dad. Whoops!

The final scene is set in the wonderful orange glow of the foundry. As the workers are being pushed harder and replaced by cheaper labour, it is down to Wong Fei Hung to help the revolution. He fights plenty of henchmen, launching into an intense series of encounters involving flaming balls and chains. This leads to the inevitable showdown with the towering bespectacled boss. You may recognise him from some of Jackie's other films as he is none other than Ken Lo (Jackie's bodyguard), standing in at the last moment. The most memorable part of their encounter features the pair battling at the edge of a pit filled with burning coal and guess who falls in? Watching Jackie scramble around the genuine coals is too much for some - not for Jackie, he did the take twice! If this was not enough, the punishment continues until, beaten by sticks and burnt, he chances upon some industrial strength alcohol and you know it's party time! By the end he is really smoking. No, really, smoking.

As a last call for kung fu made properly, *Drunken Master II* is a fitting epitaph – the camerawork, direction, music, production values and acting are fantastic, while the martial arts are nothing short of breathtaking - even if they are not in line with the real Wong Fei Hung as some sour-faced pedants have complained. While it lacks the insane superhuman feats of other new wave martial arts films (although there is some wire assistance if you look closely) its power to convince with *almost* superhuman feats makes it a winner. Many cite this film as Jackie's finest hour, a contentious statement in such an auspicious career, but it is certainly among his best.

Injury: Getting badly singed by burning coals was incredibly painful but deep down you can't help feeling it was inevitable. The industrial alcohol? It was real. Hic.

Film Rating: ✪✪✪✪✪
Chan Rating: ✪✪✪✪✪

6: Altered States

Jackie had made several attempts over the course of his career to break the lucrative American market. He was Asia's biggest star and yet could not conquer the West. The previous choice of films in America had not enabled him to shine and he had never had the degree of control that he needed. But this time, he would succeed and the whole world would be talking about Jackie Chan.

Rumble In The Bronx (1995)

Director: Stanley Tong

Cast: Jackie Chan, Anita Mui, Francoise Yip, Bill Tung

Plot: Keung (Chan) has arrived in New York from Hong Kong. His Uncle Bill is selling his supermarket to Elaine (Mui) in order to retire and get married and Keung himself has a stake in the store. However, Elaine is confronted by various protection rackets and Keung feels bad about this. Things are not improved by the local ruffians who include Nancy, the sister of wheelchair-bound Danny. But the local gangs are just punks compared to the Uzi-toting diamond thieves who are after their stash, stolen by one of the gang and hidden in Danny's wheelchair cushion. The gang begin to realise that they are out of their depth and guess who gets implicated?

Comment: *Rumble In The Bronx* was a conscious decision to try and break the American market, but this time on Jackie's terms. Setting the film in New York (it's actually Vancouver but who cares?) allows for the majority of the cast to be English speakers and hence appeal to a wider audience.

This is one hell of a film and moves at such a frenetic pace you don't have time to breathe - just gasp, wince and laugh in roughly equal measures. The whole film is a string of beautifully orchestrated set-pieces. They include the race scene, with two duelling motorcyclists running down a street of parked cars, over the cars! There's the sequence where Keung is chased by the motorcycle gang. He dives headfirst through the sunroof of a car and the pursuing motorcycle rides between his legs (OUCH! A bit close for comfort in the out-takes, this one). Keung also has to defend himself from a sustained bottle attack by the bad guys. When they ran out of sugar glass, Jackie insisted they continue with real bottles! But this is topped by an astonishing 'take on all comers' scene at the gang's den - Keung uses fridges, sofas, pool tables, pinball machines and supermarket trolleys to teach them a lesson. Chief stunt is reserved for a spectacular 'no strings attached' jump from the top of a multi-storey car park onto a postage stamp sized balcony across the road - shot as all the big stunts are from a variety of breathtaking angles.

If all of that were not enough, the climax pushes matters into the sublime as the thieves steal a hovercraft. Keung leaps onto it and tries to take over but is forced to water-ski behind it. Not that the hovercraft stops on the land, oh no, he then has to save a child (throwing her to her mother while he gets run over) steal a Lamborghini, get the bad guys and exact cartoon revenge on Mr Big. Madness.

If you do not get excited by *Rumble In The Bronx* then you are dead, there is no other explanation. The plot is insane, but the pace and the feel-good nature is infectious. They even manage to squeeze in a classic piece of cringe comedy. Our hero faces a mirror at the supermarket, unaware that it is used for one-way surveillance and that Elaine is watching him. Jackie poses with buckets, admires himself and even squeezes a spot before the awful truth is revealed. Chan classic.

Injury: Broken ankle. Glass cuts. Getting hit by a hovercraft. Squashed by a moving van and let's not forget, almost had his manhood run over by a motorbike.

Film Rating: ✪✪✪✪✪
Chan Rating: ✪✪✪✪✪

Thunderbolt (1996)

Director: Gordon Chan (with Frankie Chan, Jackie Chan & Samo Hung)
Cast: Jackie Chan, Anita Yuen, Michael Wong, Ken Lo, Chor Yuen

Plot: Jackie is a car mechanic and driver who assists the police in finding illegal modifications that have been made to everyday vehicles. Cougar is a driver with a taste for gun smuggling and money laundering. On the expressways of Hong Kong, Cougar kills a policeman and Jackie is instrumental in his arrest. Cougar kidnaps Jackie's sisters, giving his father a heart attack and wrecking his home in order to convince Jackie to race with him. Over to Japan for the big rally. Our hero must win the race, save his sisters and perhaps, just perhaps, fall in love with cute but bumbling reporter Amy.

Comment: Even a hard-working guy like Jackie has to have hobbies and his is a very expensive one – cars. Not content with putting his life on the line for your entertainment, Jackie's idea of relaxation is zooming around racing tracks, raising money for charity. The idea of a Hong Kong *Days Of Thunder* (1990) with a little budget and lots of enthusiasm seemed a perfect 'quickie' project. Once Mitsubishi and Kirin heard of the concept though, they saw a golden marketing opportunity and invested heavily in the film. Even by Jackie's standards *Thunderbolt* is sheer madness - costing a staggering HK$160 million to make. Samo was on board to choreograph the fight scenes, *Outlaw Brothers* (1989) director and composer Frankie Chan supervised the car sequences, Gordon Chan tied it all together in the exposition and Jackie was in charge of the whole affair.

Jackie plays a car mechanic whose knowledge is such that he can hear the most minor repair requirements of a car driving in the distance. Being an upstanding member of society, he helps at police roadblocks. Trouble strikes when Cougar flagrantly ignores traffic regulations, so Jackie sets off in hot pursuit. They have a *Rebel Without A Cause* (1955) style 'chicken' race, started by a remarkably well trained dove, ending with a particularly impressive crash. Cougar escapes from gaol in an intense and bloody shoot out, all with the purpose of offering Jackie a race, which he does so in a rather unusual manner. Jackie lives with his family in a two storey pre-fab building. But not for long, because Cougar and his entourage think it would be a jolly wheeze to get a crane and lift Jackie's accommodation off its perch and take him literally for a spin around his neighbourhood. When they use his house as a demolition ball, things take a frightening turn. The whole apartment comes crashing down onto him and his family.

In Japan we get the obligatory plugs for Kirin and Mitsubishi and see Jackie on the warpath. The search for his sisters leads him to the baddies' hideout in a pachinko arcade and into one of the finest fighting set-pieces you'll ever see. Jackie, incensed, starts trashing the pachinko parlour with a novelty hammer. There is a lot of glass smashing and plenty of opportunity for humans to be treated like balls, crashing off surfaces at high speed. The pace and violence is breathtaking. Then a dash to some overhanging tarpaulin for a spot of bouncing and eventually, he ends up on a huge but dangerous neon sign and warns the thugs not to approach. Do they listen? Of course not. The whole shebang collapses in slow long shot and you stare in disbelief as three crumpled forms fall down in a hail of sparks and a cascade of pachinko balls.

Given that this is a film about a car grudge match you'd expect there to be some racing and it's no disappointment. Frankie Chan knows his cars and the choreography of the stunts shines through. Sadly the quality of the race overall is sometimes a bit basic, but this was partly due to problems with the shooting schedule, location changes and the lack of available stuntmen. The real focus is on Jackie and Cougar. Their final gravel-bound, suspense-ridden race climax is wonderful and the photo finish chequered flag deserves the slow motion lavished upon it. When the race spirals outside the grounds, we are treated to a remarkable (non-Jackie) stunt. Two guys in an observation tower have a projectile car hurtle towards them. They jump off the tower just as the car crashes right through it, tumbling down to the ground. It will come as no surprise to learn that the film-makers of *Thunderbolt* had to issue an apology to the Stuntman's Union (of which Jackie is president) because of the level of injuries on the film.

Unusually, there is a sort of love interest for Jackie in the shape of reporter Amy, whose combination of intrusive journalism and naïve giggles slowly draw her into his world. Journalists have long had a rough time in Jackie's films (*Armour Of God* has a particularly harrowing scene) but despite his stony-faced assertions, he can't help falling for Amy's charms. This is despite the fact that she costs him 30 seconds in the pit and almost killed him with her I❤U distracting lap board.

There are a few problems with the film, particularly the inherent sexism of the race-track. Also be warned that *Thunderbolt* is a fairly vicious affair. Morally the film sticks with the good guy, despite Jackie's vigilante outbursts of vandalism and violence. Regardless, *Thunderbolt* isn't the unmitigated disaster that some commentators like to think – it's a rockin' good ride of a film which certainly doesn't drag.

Film Rating: ✪✪✪
Chan Rating: ✪✪✪✪

Police Story 4 (aka Jackie Chan's First Strike) (1996)

Director: Stanley Tong

Cast: Jackie Chan, Bill Tung, Annie Wu, Jackson Lau, Yuri Petrov

Plot: Jackie is given a job by the CIA to watch Natasha on her journey to the Ukraine but becomes embroiled in a devious plan to smuggle nuclear weapons to a group of terrorists. Ending up in Australia, matters escalate as Jackie, now searching for Annie Chow's brother who has the devices, becomes implicated in the murder of her father. He needs to find the bomb, convince everyone that he is innocent and catch the real baddies. But as time ticks on, the stakes are getting higher...

Comment: Again designed to appeal to a world-wide audience, the fourth official film in the *Police Story* series divided die hard fans. Stanley Tong's international approach to the film owes more than a nod to the James Bond franchise, although Jackie's character is far more likeable than the arrogant 007. The problem with the film is twofold. Firstly, by being a pastiche of an established series, it runs the risk of being engulfed with audience expectations. Secondly, the film bears no major resemblance to the first three films. To add insult to injury, Jackie's character acquired the name Jackie instead of Ka-Kui.

We've already seen Jackie sneak around like a pro by the time we get to the first set-piece. Wearing a cute seal hat and very little else, our operative has snowskied his way past a sign showing someone being shot ("It's just for kids" he is reassured) and has set up an attack. But he is spotted and jumps from snowski to snowboard with enemies in hot pursuit. These are mad men – they are dropped, in skis, from passing helicopters to chase our hero, they crash into trees and shoot at the poor guy – his only means of escape is to jump onto a helicopter from a cliff. If this wasn't enough they bazooka the helicopter, Jackie dropping into the icy water with the burning vehicle crashing inches from him. Then, just to be sure, they shoot at him! Exhausted, he lays on the ice like Lillian Gish in *Way Down East*

(1920), only wearing less.

All through the film Jackie performs a variety of subtle little jumps and climbs. The best example of this is when he is attacked in his Australian apartment. He gets to run, jump, walk across water and crouch precariously on a very high ledge. He trashes a lovely apartment complete with koala bear and a selection of bugged clothes. Speaking of koalas and clothes, Jackie's comedy underpants are a joy to behold, even more so when he has to remove them and suffer the indignities of passing female tourists.

Cause of many a retake is a classic Jackie fight. Following accusations that he murdered their father, Jackie appeals to the grieving family, protesting his innocence. But they lay into him. They go for a multiple attack and even use weapons, so Jackie is forced to defend himself with a broom which he does with lightning rapidity and a real sense of comedy. An incredible sequence involving a ladder follows (many were broken during the shoot – you can see one crumpling in the out-takes) which Jackie dives into, out of, twirls, hits and eventually sits on, exhausted. The climax is one long roller-coaster chase. Beginning with Jackie in costume and stilts at the funeral, and with Annie held at gunpoint, he uses his leg extensions to kick the gun out of her abductor's hand, despite the fact that they are a storey higher up than him! All trails eventually lead to the swimming bath and the battle commences underwater. In a remarkably silly but enjoyable routine, Jackie takes on all comers in shark-infested waters, culminating in a thumb-sucking fight to try and stem the flow of shark-attracting blood!

The strange thing about *First Strike* is the way that it taps into so many other films for its sources, and most of them are decidedly not Hong Kong. Apart from the obvious nods to James Bond movies, there's a wonderful umbrella routine that is from Hitchcock's *Foreign Correspondent* (1940) and the sequence where the ice cracks underneath foot is foreshadowed by the line "Package for Alexander Nevsky" from Eisenstein's 1938 Russian classic. If anything, it is this that many Jackie fans bemoan – the film relies so heavily on Western imagery it may as well be a Western film. This is to miss the point – after all Jackie is not James Bond. He's given the gadgets but they are never used by him and he isn't automatically a master of everything he does.

First Strike is fun, fast and lean. It's a great family feel-good film with gasps, comedy, action and Jackie's bottom. It's not his best, most violent or serious and doesn't have his best stunts, fights or set-pieces but put together it's a cracking package that never drags.

Injury: The ladder collapsed and he was knocked unconscious.

Film Rating: ✪✪✪✪

Chan Rating: ✪✪✪✪

Mr Nice Guy (1997)

Director: Samo Hung

Cast: Jackie Chan, Richard Norton, Gabrielle Fitzpatrick, Miki Lee

Plot: TV superchef Jackie bumps into a woman escaping from the Mafia. A videotape of a huge cocaine deal is at stake and nothing will stop the bad guys from retrieving it, including kidnapping our hero's girlfriend Miki. Jackie finally faces the big cigar smoking boss to put an end to this madness, only problem is our hero is tied up and his trusty wok is nowhere to be seen.

Comment: After a fairly grim opening, *Mr Nice Guy* turns into an amiable romp around Melbourne, taking the landmarks and gangsters in its stride. Jackie is great as a superchef, adding another skill to his seemingly endless repertoire as he cooks up some mean main meals. This is above all else a foody film, from the tasty noodles at the opening, the market stalls and some utter madness with spaghetti, this is not a film to watch on an empty stomach. When Jackie demonstrates his pancake making skills at a local shopping centre, he flings pieces of the scrumptious results into the opening mouths of the grateful shoppers. However, one portion ends not in the mouth of an anticipatory spectator, but into the jaws of one of the mobsters. His next portion isn't so tasty - a handful of red hot chillies!

Naturally the film excels in the many set-pieces and chase sequences, including a chase through a wedding reception and mall brawl. Jackie and Miki also steal a twin horsed cart and career off with the baddies in tow. Jackie kicks the thugs into cafés and fruit stalls, dodging trams and overhanging signs, while the hapless Miki tries to control the runaway beasts, panicking wildly. Poor Miki, she's later captured by the Aryans and Jackie has to leap to the rescue. Perhaps to try and even the score after *City Hunter*, Richard Norton decides to level the playing field in the big fight, by having Jackie roped to four muscley guys, all pulling back his punches. Naturally, our hero lands a fair few and gets some acrobatics in for good measure, but he has to resort to using heavy machinery to get his revenge.

Mr Nice Guy is a simple chase tale and works well because of it. It makes an ideal introduction for the uninitiated but the enjoyment lies with the relentless pace of the set-pieces instead of sophisticated comic timing. Indeed much of the film seems to be a collection of re-runs from earlier films: *Police Story*'s escalators and glass, *Police Story II*'s sign dodging, the chilli gag from *Project A II*, the three girl international appeal of *Operation Condor* and so on. Although the film didn't make a loss, it failed to be the biggest film in 1997 and marked a decline in the fortunes of Hong Kong films on home territory – a non-Asian film topped the box office for the first time ever - the lamentably poor *The Lost World* (1997). Indeed, many key players (Hark, Woo, Lam, Wong) were turning to Hollywood to supplement or supplant their Hong Kong careers.

Film Rating: ✪✪✪
Chan Rating: ✪✪✪✪

My Story (1998)

Plot: The life and films of Jackie Chan, from bouncing baby to *An Alan Smithee Film*, with interviews, clips and anecdotes from the man himself and some of his many associates.

Comment: The '100% Official' documentary about Chan's life and films puts a halt on the flow of unofficial ones (*Jackie Chan: From Stuntman To Superstar* et al). Naturally, with such a long fascinating life, it can't fail to engage and entertain. There's a lot to see - Jackie as a child actor in his early roles, the bits where Bruce Lee gets to thump him in *Fist Of Fury* and *Enter The Dragon* (helpfully highlighted) and even some commercials. We are also shown Jackie's ten worst injuries, catch some fight scenes that are normally cut in the West and also see the differences between the Glickenhaus and Chan cuts of *The Protector* - riveting. Unfortunately, the time restraints mean that when intriguing lines of questioning appear, like the explanation of his editing style, or the complex camera set ups on *Miracles*, they are rushed. As an introduction to an audience who think *Rumble In The Bronx* is his first film this is ideal, but would be great to see Jackie talk about his art unencumbered by the adage that he 'just' makes action films.

Injury: Loads, but they were all from previous films.
Film Rating: ✪✪✪
Chan Rating: ✪✪

My Stunts (1998)

Director: Jackie Chan

Cast: Jackie Chan, Jackie's Stunt Team

Plot: Jackie takes us behind the scenes as he reveals the tricks of his trade - the training, the choreography, the editing and those crazy stunts – illustrated by copious clips from his films as well as providing new demonstrative sequences for deconstruction and analysis.

Comment: Companion piece to *My Story*, this is a far more satisfying affair. Jackie does the talking in his inimitable and animated fashion, making for fascinating viewing – when he describes action and technique he shows us too. Where else would you see the presenter discussing the difficulties of hanging from a moving bus with an umbrella (*Police Story*) while hanging from a moving bus by an umbrella?

Key to this documentary is the juxtaposition of short clips from Jackie's films that show the same point. His basic mat work is illustrated by numerous clips of people falling painfully, particularly during the extensive account on the set of *Who Am I?* We also get to see how Jackie forms his ideas in his 'Stunt Lab,' catch his clippings collection and his secret wall montage. Additionally, there are specially filmed stunt sequences that have been deconstructed as far as shot and technique are concerned. The equipment used may be primitive but the results are astounding – the mutual respect between Jackie and his stunt team shines out.

Unlike most 'Making Of…' documentaries, *My Stunts* does not destroy the illusion on screen. If anything it enhances it. As a testament to Jackie and his stunt team's work it is second to none, and as an inspiration to low budget filmmakers it's essential.

Film Rating: ✪✪✪✪
Chan Rating: ✪✪✪✪

Who Am I? (1998)

Director: Benny Chan and Jackie Chan

Cast: Jackie Chan, Michelle Ferre, Mira Yamamoto

Plot: A crack team of anonymous international commandos steal a powerfully explosive rock. But they are set up and all killed bar one – and he has lost his memory. Helped by a local African tribe, Whoami (Jackie) eventually finds his way out of the desert only to find himself pursued for something he can't quite remember. His quest for self-discovery takes him from South Africa to Holland. With international arms deals, a disk of secrets, three kidnapped scientists and his past life a blank, Whoami must rely on the help of Agent Morgan, Christine the reporter, and demon driver Yuki to restore order. But are they all his friends?

Comment: Jackie had come up with the idea for an amnesia film and a kung fu western some time before, and you can understand he was not impressed when Samo's next picture turned out to be an amnesiac kung fu western - the hugely entertaining *Once Upon A Time In China & America* (aka *Once Upon A Time In China 6*, 1998) - resulting in *Who Am I?* appearing to be a second hand idea. He needn't have worried, because the interest lies in the spectacle rather than plot similarities. Jackie's own kung fu western is hoped to premiere for Chinese New Year 2000 – the wittily named *Shanghai Noon*.

As Whoami, Jackie gets to abseil from helicopters and utilise some great glue guns as part of his mission. The start is explosive and incoherent, but sets Jackie up with the major MacGuffin that will underpin the rest of the film - his amnesia. Jackie's tribal make-up is great as he goes back to the wild. Coming across a rallying duo where the man has been poisoned, Whoami does the decent thing by neutralising the wound and setting up an IV drip using some coconuts, before completing the race in impressive time.

After Jackie escapes from Mr Morgan - throwing himself out of a building tied up with rope and twirling his way down (handcuffed incidentally), he teams up with Christine and Yuki and the three get involved in an *Italian Job* (1969) style car chase. Yuki's remarkable driving skills, especially when parking, have to be seen to be believed. Then it's off to Holland to try and unravel more clues. This part contains one of the best sequences since the *Project A* films. After tipping off the bad guys, revealing his location and discovering Christine is not a reporter but a CIA agent, Jackie flees the café onto the streets of Rotterdam, thugs in hot pursuit. He faces his assailants without the aid of shoes, and they keep stamping on his feet. What he needs is quality footwear and, as it's Holland, he finds a clog stall. Cue lots of slipping, kicking and flipping clogs at the henchmen in a beautifully choreographed sequence. There are also some house removals going on in that street and, as the furniture is dangling precariously above the alley, you can guess what's coming. In clogs, our hero dodges falling pianos and sofas, clutching a puppy that he has rescued from certain death! Awesome.

Eventually, Jackie breaks into Morgan's high rise modernist lair and sets about getting the disk, simultaneously upsetting the electronic transfer of money by re-routing it to the Save The Children fund. He escapes to the rooftop and the stage is set for the showdown. You can see from the out-takes that they really were crazy enough to set up a fight at such altitude. They spar at the edge of the building which leads to the all important disc spiralling down to the car park. So, after dispatching the thugs, Jackie has to run down the side of the building to retrieve it. You did read that right. Starting at the top of a ridiculous glass covered incline, Jackie runs and slides his way to the bottom.

Who Am I? contains some of Jackie's best sequences but ultimately the film is a bit flat. Though by no means a disaster, the need to appeal to an English speaking audience and the cardboard characterisation (character complexity being measured by how many levels of double-crossing you are involved in) relegate this to an enjoyable but minor work.

Film Rating: ✪✪
Chan Rating: ✪✪✪✪

Jackie had not made a film for a US director in 15 years, but he and Willie were convinced by Brett Ratner that his script for

Rush Hour had the potential to be a hit. The film made over $33 million on its opening weekend alone and proved a monster smash world-wide. Jackie had become, officially, a superstar in America. The success of *Rush Hour*, the rise of his autobiography *I Am Jackie Chan* to the top of the best-seller lists, and the long overdue acceptance of his genius in the West has tended to cloud people's vision of this film. It had a budget of $35 Million (US) – you could make *Miracles*, *Police Story I & II* and *Operation Condor* together for the same price.

Rush Hour (1998)

Director: Brett Ratner

Cast: Jackie Chan, Chris Tucker, Ken Leung, Chris Penn, Elizabeth Peña, Michael Chow, Julia Hsu, Lucy Lin, Roger Fan, George Cheung

Plot: Consul Chan's daughter Su Yung is kidnapped by Chung Tao's evil gang with a $50 million price tag for her return. Chan wants top Hong Kong cop Lee (Jackie) to investigate, but the FBI want him out of the way so partner him with LAPD buffoon James Carter (Tucker). Our heroes learn about each other's cultures and try to rescue the girl, but with explosives and Uzi-totting criminals to contend with, will they succeed?

Comment: When we first meet Jackie, recovering ancient Chinese artefacts from some unscrupulous villains in a Hong Kong harbour, the prospects don't look too bad. He displays his custom agility, slipping in through tight windows, beating up criminals and dodging a cargo crate within inches of death. In America though, Jackie spends most of his time evading Chris Tucker, and frankly who can blame him? After climbing onto a bus the hard way he is caught again, only to catch onto a hanging sign and drop off that onto a passing lorry. Now that sounds pretty exciting, but this one has him hanging there like a smoking mackerel before dropping onto a virtually stationary truck from the height of about five inches. There is no attempt at spectacle, suspense or even gratuitous editing. There are a couple of nuggets to latch onto - Jackie breaking into the Consul's house is typically impressive, but these moments are few and far between. There are a few short fights - Jackie takes on some ruffians in a bar after he has made a 'rib tickling' cultural faux pas. Later he rescues Carter and the two fight together, producing an adequate blend of Chan's choreography and high-fiving buddy flick. Best of the bunch though sees Jackie fighting while trying to prevent the artefacts from being smashed, with all the enhanced expressions and punch 'n' catch silliness that we have come to know and love.

Chan's big stunt comes, naturally, at the film's climax. Having let the evil Brit traitor fall to his doom in a tension-free scene, our hero is left dangling precariously from a high beam at the Cultural Centre. But fear not, for Chris Tucker is on hand with a useful flag for Jackie to slide down, which he duly does. Slowly.

The first problem is Chris Tucker, the man who single-handedly ruined Luc Besson's *The Fifth Element* (1997). Not content to have the most pitiful whining voice and irritating dance manoeuvres known to human kind, Mr Tucker also revels in embarrassingly crass sexism ("move along titties") and racism ("you no speaky de Engerlish?") – the latter 'justified' by a throwaway line at the film's close. Director Brett Ratner sensibly decided that this was not to be the film that Jackie died on. As a result, Jackie stands around for most of the time waiting for something to happen. They let Jackie do the stunt choreography, but with an American co-ordinator supervising. The shooting schedules on this film were incredibly tight. Chan is used to spending up to three months shooting a fight routine, but given just a morning to come up with a sequence from scratch is impossible. That the sequences have any merit at all is a credit to his tolerance as much as his choreography.

We know that you may well have bought this book on the basis of seeing *Rush Hour*, it was a huge hit all over the world and will hopefully see Jackie get the roles he deserves in the West. However, this is a dull and irritating film. If you like Jackie in this, then you ain't seen nothing yet – go out and treat yourself to one of his other films. You will not regret it. Promise.

Film Rating: ✪

Chan Rating: ✪✪

Gorgeous (1999)

Director: Vincent Kok

Cast: Jackie Chan, Tony Leung, Hsu Qi, Emil Chau

Plot: Ah Bu is an innocent Taiwanese girl with an affinity for dolphins and fairy tales. One day she finds a message of love in a bottle from Albert, a man in Hong Kong. Leaving her family and doting suitor LongYi, she makes for the city. She locates Albert, but discovers that the message was for his boyfriend. Ah Bu spots rich businessman CN Chan (Jackie) on a yacht and saves him following a confrontation with his old school rival LW Lu. The two start dating, but will true love run the happiest course, or will Ah Bu return to Taiwan a dejected but wiser soul?

Comment: *Rush Hour* must have been a confusing time for Jackie - the shoot spent more time on the dialogue than his action scenes, resulting in a double whammy of not enough time and a patronising film crew to contend with. Yet it became his biggest financial success. Rather than launch straight into another unsuitable role, Chan returned to Hong Kong but as the plot summary above should indicate, this is not an action film at all - it's a gentle love story.

The film hinges on Ah Bu's adventure to find her dream love. She is more than your average idealist, she has an empathy with aquatic life that is in tune with her name - from a fairy story about two lovers who turn into dolphins. Her joie de vivre liberates all those whom she touches but she also represents the quality of innocence unprotected, her very survival depends on her naiveté. Jackie is CN Chan, a stupidly rich businessman who can buy anything or anyone he wants, but has reached that middle-aged crisis whereby his life has become meaningless. He becomes infatuated with Bu's lack of inhibition, but ultimately is still too tied to his world to appreciate her feelings until she is gone. Jackie plays the role with aplomb, relishing the opportunity to relax a while and just act. Not of course that this doesn't leave room for some fighting. The ethos of the film's violence is "Losing with dignity, winning with pride" but that is not to say that there aren't a number of exhilarating sequences to watch.

The main source of fight action involves Jackie facing a lighter professional fighter hired by LW to defeat him. The point is to humiliate him as, even if he wins, there will be no joy in defeating a lighter man. This also distances CN from a direct one-on-one conflict with LW which would upset the tone by being too aggressive. Alan the boxer is a great character and played by well-known martial artist Brett Alan. What makes him interesting is that he is not your standard rent-a-heavy, but a tough lithe fighter who is given the added bonus of some bizarre character traits.

Director Vincent Kok brings a glowing, gliding touch to the proceedings. He favours slow steadicam shots to give the film a breezy feel. Comparisons with Jackie's other films occur in the details. The girl swinging fight routines from *Half A Loaf Of Kung Fu* and *City Hunter* make two welcome reprises here, although not in the way you'd expect. Jackie makes his love for Fred Astaire films shine on celluloid when Ah Bu and CN dance together.

Gorgeous is a sweet, saccharine, snuggles-on-the-sofa film that makes you grin with its infectious niceness. You'll laugh, you'll have a little sniff and you'll go "aaahhh" a lot. If you can get hold of a copy you're in for a real treat. This is clearly a good direction for Jackie to be aiming for; he is approaching 50 (though you'd never know it) and there is a limit to how much the human body can take. The cumulative effect of a lifetime of knocks and broken bones is huge and Jackie's skills have not diminished over the years, they've matured. Now is perhaps the ideal time for him to be moving into a new phase that combines his skills as an actor, director, artist and innovator.

Injury: Alas even the relatively cushioned environment of the romantic comedy could not save Jackie from injury – his hip was injured by a motorbike which was stationary at the time. Another injury could be to his macho-man image – remember, no one leaves a Jackie film before the credits have finished rolling, so check out the very last shot of the film. Aaaah.

Film Rating: ✪✪✪✪✪
Chan Rating: ✪✪✪

7: Also Showing.....

Jackie has also been involved with other aspects of film making and has been credited on many more films. In his early days, he was involved with a lot of action/stunt choreography and later on, when his bank balance had increased, became a producer too. Now a star, he has naturally been asked to appear in many cameo roles. Here is a selection of other credits:

Jackie As Producer

Jackie set up his own production company Golden Way, which is a subsidiary of Golden Harvest. It gave him the opportunity to make high quality films and also give up-and-coming actors a break in the industry.

Naughty Boys (1986) saw him produce and arrange the stunts, as well as appearing in a cameo capacity. It also got him connected with his personal bodyguard Ken Lo.

I Am Sorry (1987) Co producer

Rouge (1988) A young modern couple help Fleur, a tragic ghost, find her lover who was meant to have died in a suicide pact with her at the turn of the century. Starring Anita Mui and Leslie Cheung, *Rouge* is worthy of your attention because it is one of the few true classics of modern cinema. This tragic story of love, loss and the inability of modern times to relate to eternal devotion, is an elegiac lament for times past - more cruel maybe, but better. It is to Jackie's credit that he financed this delicate film from Stanley Kwan who is such a talented director.

The Inspector Wears Skirts I and *II* (1988/9) with Cynthia Rothrock and Sibelle Hu respectively.

Stagedoor Johnnie (1990) was another showcase for Anita Mui, its 1930s setting allowed easy use of the sets built for *Miracles*.

Centre Stage aka *Actress* (1990) Stanley Kwan directed another period piece for Jackie. Starring Maggie Cheung, it was critically acclaimed but failed to get distribution in the West.

The Shootout (1992)

Stunt/Action Choreographer

This was the role to which young Jackie aspired all those years ago. Little did he know that he could achieve so much more. It is worth noting that the following films are those for which his only role was action co-ordinator - he has naturally been involved with the action work on all the films in which he has starred!

The Young Dragons (1973)
The Dragon Tamers (1975)
Dance Of Death aka *The Eternal Conflict* (1976)
The Iron Fisted Monk (1977) Samo's directorial debut
The Odd Couple aka *Dance Of Death* (1979)
36 Crazy Fists (1980) Often sold on the basis that this is a Jackie Chan film, it is nothing of the sort. Jackie did some stunt choreography and an unscrupulous devil took behind the scenes footage of him at work. Jackie is constantly puffing on a cigarette (a habit he has now given up, although it was considered essential for stuntmen to be chain-smokers at the time) and occasionally waves his arms a bit. Riveting.

The Outlaw Brothers (1989) directed by composer Frankie Chan, a fine action film with Yakuri Oshima and Nishimi Michenko.

Cameo Appearances

Hapkido (1972) starring Samo Hung and Angela Mao Ying
Golden Lotus (1974)
Ninja Wars (1982) Directed by Mitsumisa Saito and starring Sonny Chiba, who has had a long career as a karate action hero, most famously in the hyper-violent *Street Fighter* films of the 1970s. Like Jackie, his longevity is astounding for such a physical actor. Jackie's cameo whets the appetite for what could be a cracking (bones!) buddy movie if the two ever teamed up.
Two In A Black Belt (1984)
Pom Pom (1985) Jackie and Yuen Biao reprised their roles from the Lucky Stars series for Samo's comedy about some barmy detectives.
The Kid From Tibet (1991) Yuen Biao's directorial debut, where he also stars as a mystical monk.
Project S (aka *Supercop II*) (1992) Jackie reprises his *Police Story* character in a totally incongruous, yet hilarious cameo. Disguised as a woman, complete with the ultimate in comedy breasts, he apprehends a similarly dressed jewellery thief. He hitches his skirt up, then throws himself over several cars. Classic.

Burn, Hollywood, Burn (aka *An Alan Smithee Film*) (1997) Jackie was persuaded by his friend and co-star Sylvester Stallone to take the film as a quick way to enhance his star presence in the States. He plays …Jackie Chan and is interviewed about his role in Alan Smithee's film *Trio*, and is featured enjoying the highlife. He denies that he dies in the picture ("Jackie Chan never die," he declares – although we know he has done in the past, right?). Jackie fits perfectly into the picture's spirit and camps his star status to the max.

King Of Comedy (1999) Jackie makes a brief appearance as an extra who shows Steven Chow Sing Chi how to take a fall in this funny and yet strangely bizarre romantic comedy. Chow returned the favour by appearing as the policeman in *Gorgeous*.

8: So, You Want To Know More?

Books

I Am Jackie Chan, Jackie Chan with Jeff Yang, ISBN 0-345-42913-3

Jackie's autobiography is a must have. A fascinating and compelling tale, particularly of his formative years and his relationship with the other Little Fortunes.

Jackie Chan: Inside The Dragon, Clyde Gentry III, ISBN 0-87833-970-1

Lavishly illustrated and fascinating book, it also tries to focus on the more serious side to Jackie's film making. Highly Recommended.

The Essential Jackie Chan Sourcebook, Jeff Rovin & Kathy Tracy, ISBN 0-671-00843-9

Trade paperback size book covering all the major bases. A bit eclectic but the enthusiasm shines through.

Dying For Action: The Life And Films Of Jackie Chan, Renee Witterstaetter, ISBN 0-09-186452-6

A case of throwing everything you can get your hands on into one book. The results are varied.

Hong Kong Cinema: The Extra Dimension, Stephen Teo, ISBN 0-85170-514-6

A brave stab at serious criticism, this may be a bit heavy for the casual browser but is essential for tracing of the roots of Hong Kong cinema and its cultural themes.

Hong Kong Babylon, Fredric Dannen & Barry Long, ISBN 0-571-19040-5

It may look chunky but this is a surprisingly quick read. Basically a history, a bit of gossip, some interviews and a lot of capsule reviews. A good introduction.

Hong Kong Action Cinema, Bey Logan, ISBN 1-85286-540-7

Thorough and impressive book from *Impact* magazine's Bey Logan. This covers everything from bloodshed to fantasy, comedy to swordplay. Stunningly illustrated, partly in colour, there is a whole chapter on Jackie alone. Highly recommended.

Video Availability

Jackie's films are wide spectacles so ideally the cinema is the place to see him at his best. Unfortunately this is all but impossible bar the odd 'cult' screening and his more recent hits. Video availability comes and goes but below is a list of the most recent catalogue numbers for Jackie's films. Be warned that many are dubbed, cut (either by the BBFC or the distributors or just because it's a bad print) and/or pan and scanned which seriously diminishes the impact - the worst offender is *Miracles* which has lost half an hour, half the screen and is horribly dubbed. Many DVD players are compatible with the old VCD format and these can be found in some Chinese supermarkets or over the internet - the aforementioned *Miracles* on VCD is a far more satisfying affair, in widescreen and subtitled. UK DVD availability will improve with time (although the Hong Kong release of *Gorgeous* is just that - gorgeous - and packed with extras too) but currently most are lacklustre English language versions. Only *Rush Hour* stands out as an exemplary DVD, it's a pity it's such a poor film! Also beware if renting some of the older films from video shops. Many, many films have been rehashed or retitled given Chan's subsequent fame. The worst offender we came across was the video labelled *The Young Tiger*, which contained a plot summary of *Eagle Shadow Fist*, and turned out to be *Police Woman/ Rumble In Hong Kong*!

36 Crazy Fists SUD2172
Armour Of God (Widescreen) HK073
Big Brawl, The (Battle Creek Brawl) VC3238
Burn Hollywood Burn EVS1328
City Hunter VIA7578
Crime Story VIA7581
Dragon Fist JC001
Dragon Lord (Widescreen) V3525
Dragons Forever (Widescreen) V3554
Drunken Master (Widescreen) HK012
Eagle Shadow Fist TGI0002
Fantasy Mission Force TGI0003
Fearless Hyena JC003
Fearless Hyena 2 TGI0005
Fire Dragon KIS97015 (DVD) PAR61017
First Mission, The VPD361
Half A Loaf Of Kung Fu TGI0006
Hand Of Death V3427
Heart Of Dragon (Widescreen) V3552
Island On Fire VIA7560
Jackie Chan - From Stuntman To Superstar IMC186
Jackie Chan - Mister Nice Guy EVV1312 (DVD) EDV9032

Jackie Chan - My Story VIA7603

Jackie Chan - My Stunts VIA7604

Jackie Chan - Shaolin Wooden Men KIS97005 (DVD) PAR61018

Jackie Chan - The Young Tiger KIS97013 (DVD) PAR61016

Jackie Chan's First Strike EVS1260 (DVD) EDV9007

Killer Meteors, The TGI0008

Magnificent Bodyguards TGI0009

Magnificent Bodyguards / Fantasy Mission Force JC007

Master With Cracked Fingers VIA7601

Miracles - The Canton Godfather ONE00705

My Lucky Stars (Widescreen) V3556

New Fist Of Fury JC002

Operation Condor - Armour Of God 2 (Widescreen) EVS1082

Police Story (Widescreen) HK055

Police Story 2 (Widescreen) HK056

Police Story 3 VIA7569

Project A (Widescreen) HK069

Project A II (Widescreen) HK070

Project S (Widescreen) V3566 (DVD) DV1006

Protector, The S011538

Rumble In Hong Kong (Police Woman) V3471

Rumble In The Bronx D969570

Rush Hour (Widescreen) EVS1352 (DVD) EDV9014

Snake And Crane Arts Of Shaolin TGI0013

Snake In The Eagle's Shadow (Widescreen) HK011

Spiritual Kung Fu TGI0012

To Kill With Intrigue TGI0007

Twin Dragons ONE00701

Twinkle Twinkle Lucky Stars EH0042

Wheels On Meals (Widescreen) V3558

Winners And Sinners VPD371

Young Master, The (Widescreen) V3465

Web Resources

Naturally with a star of Jackie's stature there are a plethora of sites out there all vying for your attention. Search engines will often have their own Jackie Chan subdirectory for you to browse. For 'word searches' it is often better to try the less well known films or face hundreds of thousands of matches. The sites below are a good starting point and chosen not only for content but for browser compatibility.

The Official Jackie Chan Web Page - http://www.jackie-chan.com/

Jackie's own publicity and fan club page with plenty to see for the non-member and links to buy Jackie merchandise. Easy design, all the news direct from source and exclusive pictures. This should be your first port-of-call.

Jackie Chan Connection - http://www.jcconnection.com/

Differs from many sites in its laudable aim to provide information on Jackie normally ignored in the West. There are lots of articles in the Hong Kong press to read (the one on *Rush Hour* is great), pictures of exhibitions, shows and TV appearances and video clips of adverts.

Chan News Online - http://www.geocities.com/Tokyo/Bridge/5767/main.htm

All the latest news and rumours culled from newsgroups. The wealth of information and speed of loading makes up for the basic design.

Jackie Chan - The Man & His Music - http://www.geocities.com/Tokyo/Pagoda/6094/

We've not had the space to discuss Jackie's singing career so why not go to this really nice little site and find out more?

Becoming The Dragon - http://www.jackiechan.net/

Professional looking clean site with lots of thought and factual details.

Fanclubs

Jackie Chan International Fan Club

145 Waterloo Road

Kowloon

Hong Kong

If you wish to contact any of the regional fan clubs, go to www.jackie-chan.com for details

The Essential Library

If you've enjoyed this book why not try the following titles in the Pocket Essentials library?

The Slayer Files: Buffy the Vampire Slayer by Peter Mann - Complete episode guide and cast information on the hit TV series of the millennium featuring the most beautiful girl on the planet.

Woody Allen by Martin Fitzgerald – Follow his life from desperate comedian to tragic dramatist.

Jackie Chan by Michelle Le Blanc & Colin Odell (March 2000) – Every broken bone dissected, every stupendous stunt analysed, and every action movie reviewed.

The Brothers Coen by John Ashbrook & Ellen Cheshire – The curious charm of the modern Brothers Grimm, from *Blood Simple* to *The Big Lebowski*.

Film Noir by Paul Duncan (April 2000) – Films of trust and betrayal, from *Double Indemnity* to *Touch Of Evil*.

Heroic Bloodshed edited by Martin Fitzgerald (March 2000) – Hong Kong Action Cinema, where only the bullets are faster than the subtitles! Features interviews with John Woo and Wong Kar-Wai.

Alfred Hitchcock by Paul Duncan – He spent his life creating public unease with *Psycho*, *Vertigo*, *Rear Window* and 50 more films. Find out how Hitch did it.

Stanley Kubrick by Paul Duncan – *Eyes Wide Shut* was only the latest in a long line of controversial films by the director's director.

David Lynch by Michelle Le Blanc & Colin Odell – Close your minds to the surreal, violent world of *Twin Peaks* and *Wild At Heart*. Open your hearts to the beauty of *The Elephant Man* and *The Straight Story*.

Noir Fiction by Paul Duncan (April 2000) – On your travels down the dark highways of fiction you will meet James M Cain, Cornell Woolrich, Jim Thompson, David Goodis, Charles Willeford, James Ellroy, Derek Raymond and many troubled souls.

Orson Welles by Martin Fitzgerald – He made the best American film ever made, *Citizen Kane*, and then got better! Discover how.

Available at all good bookstores at £2.99 each, order online at
www.pocketessentials.com, or send a cheque to:
Pocket Essentials (Dept JC), 18 Coleswood Rd, Harpenden, Herts, AL5 1EQ, UK
Please make cheques payable to 'Oldcastle Books.' Add 50p postage & packing for each book in the UK and £1 elsewhere.
US customers should contact Trafalgar Square Publishing on 802-457-1911 (Tel), 802-457-1913 (Fax), e-mail: tsquare@sover.net